The ART of SHELLING

A complete guide to finding shells and other beach collectibles at shelling locations from Florida to Maine

By
Chuck Robinson
Debbie Robinson

Illustrations by
April Wengren

D0920651

Cover Design and Photography by
Chuck and Debbie Robinson

Second Edition, Completely Revised

Old Squan Village Publishing
Manasquan, New Jersey

594
ROB

The ART of SHELLING

**A complete guide to finding shells
and other beach collectibles at
shelling locations from Florida to Maine**

By
**Chuck Robinson
Debbie Robinson**

Illustrations By April Wengren

Published by: *Old Squan Village Publishing*
18 Willow Way
Manasquan, NJ 08736-2835 USA

Copyright © 1995, 2000
by Chuck Robinson and Debbie Robinson
First Printing 1995
Second Printing 2000, completely revised
Printed in the United States of America

Publisher's Cataloging in Publication Data
Robinson, Chuck.
The art of shelling: a complete guide to finding shells and other beach collectibles at shelling locations from Florida to Maine / by Chuck Robinson and Debbie Robinson.
p.   cm.
Includes bibliographical references and index.
1. Shells. 2. Shells—Atlantic Coast (US)—Collectors and collecting.
I. Title. II. Robinson, Debbie.
Library of Congress Card Number: 00-190216
594—dc21
ISBN 0-9647267-8-5 $14.95 pbk.

Contents

List of Illustrations, Tables, and Maps

Introduction

The Art of Shelling is a shell hunting guidebook. It is interesting reading for everyone who loves seashells and the seashore environment. The book explains what shells are and details specifically where and how to find them. The information is presented in an enjoyable and easy-to-read format. After learning about each location, you will feel as though you had actually been there.

This completely revised second edition of *The Art of Shelling* is our way of sharing what we have learned during more than fifteen years of intensive seashore travel, beach exploration, and mollusk study.

Use *The Art of Shelling* as a guide to the areas mentioned. Take this book with you on your excursions as a reference source. Utilize the information provided to find new places to explore. Please obey local laws concerning the collecting of shells. We ask that you never take live mollusks.

Disclaimer Notice

PART ONE:
AN INTRODUCTION TO SHELLING

1

About Shells

Shells are the supporting structures of mollusks. They also provide protection for these invertebrate animals. Mollusks have soft bodies containing internal organs. Many species have a muscular foot and some species have a head with tentacles and eyes. Scientists estimate there are 80,000-100,000 species of mollusks. Mollusks of the same species resemble each other, are capable of interbreeding, but may differ slightly in size, shell shape, and color.

Shells are primarily made of the mineral calcium carbonate, a salt present in the blood of mollusks, obtained either from the food they eat or water they live in. The one feature unique to all mollusks is the presence of a mantle. The mantle is a lobe, pair of lobes, or fold of muscular flesh containing specialized glands. The glands convert the salt in the blood to a liquid form of calcium carbonate. Cells at the edge of the mantle secrete this liquid. It solidifies, forming more shell. As mollusks grow larger and additional shell is required for support, another layer of calcium carbonate is spread onto the lip of the shell.   Since the thickness of each layer is slightly different, this starting and stopping of the growth process forms "growth lines." The lines are very prominent on the Atlantic Surf Clam and Knobbed Whelk.

Many species of mollusks found in warmer southern waters have shells more colorful than those found farther north because the southern occurring mollusks have more nutrients available to them. The organic pigments contained in the nutrients are processed by the mollusk, distributed by the blood system, then mixed with the liquid calcium just before the shell hardens. A colorful shell is produced. The colors and patterns of each species are inherited although there is some natural variation. Environment and diet also influence the coloration of shells within species.   For example, Rock Dogwinkles are normally gray or white, but become yellow when fed a diet of barnacles. When fed a diet of blue mussels, they develop purple and brown markings.

Color variation can also occur when shells buried in sand or mud absorb the color of the substrate. Also, long exposure to the sun will bleach shells, greatly changing their original appearance.

Shell Types

The two types of shells commonly found are bivalves, mollusks with two shells hinged together, and univalves, mollusks having a single shell. The four most common classes of mollusks are gastropods, bivalves, chitons, and tusks. Interestingly, octopus and squid are mollusks too, but have no external shell.

Gastropods frequently found are the snail and whelk. Gastropods (illustration 1) live in fresh and salt water and some species live on land. In most cases, their single shell

illustration 1   Gastropod

has a spiral appearance consisting of a coiled tube, increasing in size as it winds around a central axis. This mollusk uses a foot to move along the floor of its habitat. Many varieties of these single shell mollusks eat bivalves. Depending on the species, they retrieve their meal by either forcing the bivalves apart with their foot or by drilling into the bivalve's shell. An interesting experience is to pull a live whelk from the water, only to find it has pried open a cockle shell and is in the process of ingesting the flesh inside.

Bivalves inhabit oceans, brackish water, and fresh water. Examples of frequently found bivalves are the clam and scallop. The two shells of the bivalve are generally mirror images of one another, joined by an elastic ligament or hinge. The shells are described as being a right and left valve. When the mollusk is alive, the valves are attached. When the animal dies and decays and only the shell is left, the two valves usually break apart at the hinge. Occasionally, bivalves found on the beach appear to have dried seaweed on them. This is the periostracum, the outermost layer of the shell, and it may act as a form of protection and camouflage for the live mollusk.

Bivalves have four distinct appearances (illustration 2): they can be smooth; they can have a concentric sculpture–with the hinge on top, the lines going around the shell; a radial sculpture–with the hinge on top, the lines running from a central point at the hinge and radiating out

illustration 2   Bivalves: top– Concentric Sculpture, bottom left– Radial Sculpture, bottom right– Latticed Sculpture

and down the shell; or they can have a latticed sculpture–lines running in both directions. In some species, one valve differs from the other in color and shape.

On the inside of bivalves' shells you can see muscle scars.   They are circular-like indentations where the animal's muscles, used to open and close the two valves, were attached.   There are muscle scars at each end of the shell, as seen in the Atlantic Surf Clam (see illustration 23, page 114.) There is another scar located along the outer edge of the shell. This indentation is where the mantle was attached.

To feed on plankton, bivalves separate their shells and extend two tiny siphon tubes.   One tube is used to draw in water, containing three essential nutrients: oxygen, minerals, and plankton. After digesting the microscopic life, the waste is pumped out the other tube. Amazingly, oysters can process three and a half gallons of water per hour.

Most bivalves have teeth; however, these teeth have nothing to do with their eating process. The teeth are on the interior of the shell. They are located near the hinge and interlock when the mollusk closes its valves. Teeth size and patterns are essential identifiers when distinguishing similar species.

Unlike gastropods, bivalves do not have a head, jaw, or radula; they do have fine tentacles and eyes. These eyes do not "see" like a human's, but are sensitive to changes in light, helping them detect danger. When necessary to flee from predators or avoid the rough action of surf, bivalves dig into the sand with their muscular foot and bury themselves. Angel Wings and razor clams dig into sand and mud using other techniques. Angel Wings extend and wiggle their foot into the sand, then inflate the

foot with blood. This acts as an anchor. Then they pull
themselves into the sand. Razor clams squirt a jet of water
into the sand creating a hole. As they pull themselves in,
more sand washes out and the hole gets deeper. Some
bivalves, by secreting a strong acid, can burrow into solid
rock. Scallops use their excellent swimming ability as
their means of protection. When danger threatens, these
bivalves forcefully squirt water between their two valves,
blasting off, leaving behind a cloud of sand.

Two shells difficult to find are chitons and tusks. The
primitive chiton lives in a marine environment and is
bilaterally symmetrical with a long, flat body. The shell
has eight arched overlapping valves covered by spines,
scales, beads, and a leathery sheath. Tusks, a small group
of mollusks, live in very deep ocean water and resemble
miniature elephant tusks. They are tube-like, open at both
ends, with one end larger than the other. The larger
opening is oval in shape.

Mollusks have adapted to environments including
rocky shores, sandy beaches, marshes, and mangrove
swamps. Some species even live in trees, such as Liguus
Tree Snails found on smooth barked trees in the
Everglades National Park. Other snails, as seen in small
ditches along the streets near the bay in Friendship, Maine,
or in the sandy yards of cottages on Ocracoke Island,
North Carolina, are land dwellers. However, most species
of mollusks live under water where they have adapted to
environments of different temperatures, salinity, and
depths.

Mollusk Reproduction

Methods of reproduction vary greatly among
mollusks. Some mollusks are either male or female, some

contain both sexes in the same animal, while others change their sex one or more times.

Lightening Whelk are separate sexes and join together to mate. The female fertilizes the eggs internally. She starts spawning a string of egg cases six weeks after mating. It takes eight to twelve days to spawn twenty-four inches of egg cases. A nine inch whelk produces a thirty inch string. Each disk of a string contains 30-100 baby whelk. A large string of cases may contain 5,000-12,000 babies. However, only 500 may survive. Female mollusks are larger than males, because it takes more physiological energy to produce eggs than to produce sperm.

The female Common Northern Moon Shell does not make a string of cases. She takes the babies from the mantle cavity, mixes them with a gelatin-like mixture of sand, and forms a sand collar. Olives release their eggs in round capsules. They attach them to a hard object or they float free. The young escape in about a week. Tritons' eggs are laid in capsules and the female usually sits on the egg mass, sometimes for a month. Helmets lay their eggs in capsules, usually in masses, then free swimming larvae emerge. Tusk shells, chitons, some gastropods, and most bivalves discharge large numbers of eggs and sperm into the water, where fertilization takes place. This is true of the surf clam. Its larvae are free swimming for about two weeks before settling to the bottom. The larvae of some mollusks may live for one to two months in the open ocean. This may account for the wide geographic range of some species.

How Long Do Mollusks Live?

Most mollusks live for several years. The Horse

Conch, Florida's state shell and its largest shell, grows up to twenty-four inches and lives up to fifteen years. The Lightening Whelk, another large mollusk, grows to sixteen inches and lives ten to twelve years. On the other hand, some mollusks live a relatively short life. As an example, scallops live for about two years. The only way scientists can determine the exact age of a mollusk is by dissecting the animal. However, you can estimate the age of a mollusk by measuring its size and comparing it to its life span. A Lightening Whelk half its adult size would be half the age of its life span. For example, knowing the Lightening Whelk grows to sixteen inches and lives to twelve years, if you find an eight inch Lightening Whelk, you can estimate it is about six years old.

Knowing what a shell is and understanding the varied habits and environments of these creatures will help you to become an expert sheller. Instead of depending on luck, you will know what you're looking for and where to find it. *The Audubon Society Field Guide to North American Seashells*, by Harald A. Rehder, 1990, is a very helpful shell identification book. It includes 705 color photographs of shells arranged by shape and six hundred and seventy-one shells are covered in full detail with notes on 200 more.

2

Shelling Tips:
How and Where to Find Shells

Searching for and finding beautiful shells is an exciting and enjoyable experience. This chapter will explain general techniques used to find shells, techniques transferable to many different shelling locations and situations. You will also read about specific shelling locations and the shell hunting techniques proven to be successful at these locations.

The most important skill required to be a successful sheller is a keen sense of observation. You must train yourself to "narrow focus." This is accomplished by forming a mental picture of the shell you want to find and concentrating exclusively on this picture while looking for the shell. As an example, when looking for an olive shell, think about what it looks like. Picture it rolling up onto the beach and quickly rolling back again as the water retreats. Forming this image will enable you to see the olive shell almost instantly, even when it only partially appears. By being patient and looking closely for the shells you desire, in a location they are known to be, you will find them.

Experience will improve your shelling success. During your early shelling experiences, you will probably walk right over partially exposed shells, sand dollars, and other items. Often, empty-handed shellers ask us, "Where did you find that beautiful shell?" or "Where did you find all those sand dollars?" If they slowed down and concentrated on what they were looking for, they would have more shelling success. With experience you learn how shells and other beach collectibles appear in all types of beach habitats.

Shelling on Tidal Beaches

Tidal beaches have three distinct zones, and shell hunting techniques differ in each zone. The area of dry sand is the supratidal zone, extending from the base of the sand dunes to the high water line. The intertidal zone is the area of beach covered by water at high tide and exposed at low tide. The subtidal zone is the area of shallow water and breaking waves.

In the supratidal zone, the best shelling method is to stroll the beach and look around to see what lies on the sand. Always turn over mounds of seaweed to expose any hidden shells. In this zone, shells washed ashore by extremely high tides or storms may be found. Often, shells can be seen embedded in the side of sand dunes. They were deposited there, sometimes hundreds or even thousands of years ago, when the sand dune was forming. Do not dig into the dunes or in any other way destroy them or their vegetation. Sand dunes are vital to the stabilization of beaches and must be protected.

Shelling in the intertidal zone is usually more

rewarding than in the supratidal zone. Since the water rises and falls generally two times each day, shells are constantly washed ashore, uncovered, and moved up and down the beach. In most instances we have found the best time to shell hunt is as the tide is going from high to low. The most productive shelling is often done from two hours before low tide to low tide. At times, shelling can be ideal when an offshore wind is pushing the water out even farther than usual.

Take advantage of the tides by consulting a tide table. Tide tables are found in local newspapers, bait shops, and Chamber of Commerce offices in shore towns. A tide table (table 1) is a chart listing the times oceans and bays are at their lowest and highest each day. Tide tables are set up in many different ways. However, they generally list the following information in individual columns: the date, the time of the A.M. high tide, the time of the P.M. high tide, the time of the A.M. low tide, and the time of the P.M. low tide. The tide times are listed for one specific location, indicated on the chart, and the chart will show the minutes to subtract or add for other nearby locations. Again, a general rule is to shell hunt when the tide is going out, and from two hours before low tide to low tide.

Should you own a four-wheel drive vehicle, also called an off-road vehicle (ORV), do not overlook its usefulness as a shell hunting tool on the beaches you are allowed to drive on. Once you have developed your observation skills and have had success in finding shells while combing the beach on foot, you may want to add this technique. In the intertidal zone, the outgoing tide often deposits a line of shells at the high tide line. Also, many individual shells or smaller lines of shells will often be deposited between the major high tide shell line and the

MANASQUAN INLET TIDES

JUNE 1-7

Date	Low		High	
	AM	PM	AM	PM
1	11:51	-----	5:41	6:13
2	0:34	12:44	6:38	7:06
3	1:29	1:36	7:30	7:53
4	2:21	2:27	8:18	8:39
5	3:09	3:17	9:06	9:25
6	3:57	4:03	9:54	10:09
7	4:41	4:49	10:41	10:55

To adjust for local points add or subtract the time differences:

	Low	High
Asbury Park, NJ	-0:09	-0:22
Seaside Park, NJ	-0:08	-0:21
Barnegat Inlet, NJ	+0:15	-0:08

table 1   Tide Table

water's edge. With one person driving, the other can look down, out the window at this line of shells. The driver can look ahead for larger shells or shells suddenly rolling in with the waves. In an area where there are fishermen and other beachgoers, be attentive to their movement and be alert to the location of the fishermen's poles and lines. In these busy areas the driver should leave the shelling to the passenger. Obviously this method will not be good for finding small shells. However, you can experience success finding larger shells or shells with high profiles such as whelks and bonnets. Large sand dollars can also be easily spotted.

Using your ORV allows you to cover a large area in a short time, and you can easily get to beaches out of walking distance. Using a vehicle will also extend your shelling day. After you have shelled on foot for six or seven hours, your legs can get very tired. Instead of "calling it a day," get into your ORV and continue the search. Also, rainy, windy days should not be a deterrent to your shelling because you can shell hunt from the comfort of your vehicle.

Another type of intertidal zone is the rocky shore. Shelling in this zone is done while climbing on rock ledges and boulders, crawling in rock crevices, and peering into tidal pools. To be safe, wear sneakers or hiking shoes and do not walk on the very slippery algae growing on the rocks. You can experience this vertical intertidal zone when shelling on the coast of Maine.

The subtidal zone is also a rewarding shelling area. Often there is a collection of shells under the water in "the ditch," the area formed by breaking waves and movement of water. This ditch is usually a few inches deep at low tide to a few feet deep at high tide. Shells not making it up onto the beach collect here. At low tide, put on a pair of old sneakers, walk in the water, and examine this area. If the water is calm and clear, you will see shells well enough to pick out the interesting ones by hand. You can also use a scoop or sieve to gather many shells at one time. By doing this, smaller specimens you would not have otherwise seen can be collected. If you are brave, feel around with your bare feet and search for larger shells. This works very well when searching for whelk shells, but be careful of crabs, stingray, and especially lost fishing tackle.

It is always worth going out and searching for shells on exposed sandbars. Sandbars are ridges of sand built up by the tides and currents. These ridges frequently catch the shells passing over them as the tide goes out. Sandbars are often accessible by simply wading through the water. Be extremely cautious when attempting to reach a sandbar, making sure there are no deep holes or dangerous currents. Also, be attentive to the tide. If the tide is coming in, you could get stranded on the sandbar. Often, as the tide comes in, the depth of the water is only ankle deep on the sandbar, but may become many feet deep between the sandbar and the beach.

A method of shelling for experienced swimmers in the subtidal zone is snorkeling. Snorkeling in shallow water allows the sheller to see shells missed when looking through the water. Also, snorkelers can go into deeper areas to shell hunt and observe live shells.

Other Shelling Opportunities

When a bay or inlet is dredged, sand and shells are sometimes pumped onto shore. These areas can be fun to explore after the sand has dried. Search through the sand and you may find shells not commonly found on the beach.

For years there has been a mound of dredged sand on the north end, bay side, of Ocracoke, North Carolina. Here we have found tusk shells. Tusks live in deep water and usually do not make it onto shore.

Beach replenishment is the process of pumping sand from the ocean floor onto shore to expand the width of the beach. This process is most often performed for the benefit of the tourism industry. In some cases it is done to protect the developed land near the shore. Although many people enjoy the larger beaches, the process destroys the marine life and underwater environment. It does, however, provide the sheller with another area for exploration. The beach replenishment project that began in 1997 on the New Jersey shore brought common sand dollars, sharks' teeth, and the Smooth Astarte onto the beach. Before this, these beach collectibles were an unusual find on New Jersey beaches.

Opportunities also exist for finding shells away from the beach. In Florida, for example, miles away from the ocean there are many excellent fossil shell sites. Often the fossil shells can be found right on the surface in fields, along old dirt roads, and in railroad beds.

Other Shelling Tips

Very productive shelling areas are usually found at the ends of barrier islands, on inlet banks, and at the end of peninsulas. At these locations, swift moving water carries shells between the bays and oceans and deposits them on the quick forming sandbars, rapidly exposed sand flats, or on nearby beaches. When visiting an area for the first time, these locations are generally the best place to start your shelling. Also, on any beach, areas jutting out into the water and experiencing swift currents may be excellent shelling locations.

Weather often determines the success of a shelling trip. There may be few shells on the beach after several days of calm weather. However, after several days of stormy weather, many shells and other interesting beach collectibles may be found. Items often found after a storm include buoys, driftwood, massive lengths of large rope, lobster pots, coins, and even dollar bills.

3

Preparing for Your Shell Hunting Trip

This chapter supplies helpful information for planning shelling trips. It offers guidance on how to choose a shelling location and what to bring with you. It also provides information you need to know for off-road vehicle (ORV) operation. The last section of the chapter explains some necessary precautions to help make your trip a safe one.

Selecting Your Shelling Destination

The first step to selecting a shelling destination is to determine an area appealing to your interests and budget. Part Two: Shelling Destinations will help you with this process. It describes many productive shelling locations from Florida to Maine. After selecting a few locations, write to the local chambers of commerce and tourist bureaus for information. If you are interested in visiting a state park, national park, or wildlife refuge, write directly to the specific place you want to visit. The travel reference index in this book provides addresses for the locations covered in Part Two. After gathering and reviewing all pertinent information, choose a destination. Using a current road atlas, plot a course to where you are going. You should also study the atlas to increase your familiarity with the area you plan to visit.

If you have online computer access, you can gather the above information by visiting the many web pages available. They include local chambers of commerce, visitors' bureaus, national parks, state parks, weather services, and newspapers, among others.

You need to consider what the weather conditions will be at your destination. You will be spending most of your time outdoors, so being prepared for the climate is very important. Libraries have reference books containing climate information and most road atlases include climate charts. Atlas climate charts provide specific location data, including minimum and maximum daily temperatures. They also have facts about the total number of days with precipitation for each month. Reviewing this material will help you select the type of clothing needed for the trip.

Travel guidebooks are another source of important information. They contain facts about the tourist season, interesting attractions, and seasonal events. They also provide details about transportation, tours, area history, lodging, dining, and nightlife. Another very good source of advice is the area's visitor center. The material provided will be in the form of single page brochures, booklets, and newspapers. The information they contain includes calendars of activities and places of interest. Often they include coupons to restaurants and gift shops. Thoroughly reading the publications will provide you with an overall feel for the area. Other good sources of

information are daily local newspapers and phone
directories.

Identifying Needed Items

One nice thing about traveling to beach locations
during warm seasons is the convenience of packing light.
However, be sure to bring appropriate clothing for
unexpected cooler days.   When traveling to a cooler
location, be prepared with adequate warm clothing.
Wherever you go, the weather at the shore may not be the
same as the weather predicted for inland areas.   An ocean
breeze can cool things down in a hurry, and an ocean
squall can quickly dampen your trip unless you are
prepared. Bring sweatshirts, rain jackets, and a change of
clothes.

Using a checklist of essential items (table 2) helps to
organize your trip.   Items needed for comfort and safety
include hats, ultraviolet blocking sunglasses, sweatshirts,
jackets, rain gear, a cooler for food and drinks, bug
repellant, aqua-shoes or old sneakers, beach umbrella,
flash light, first aid kit, a well-supplied tool box, and
sunscreen lotions. Sunscreens come in different levels of
protection factors (PF,) with ratings from PF2 to over
PF35.   Higher ratings provide greater protection.
Sunscreens are also available in sensitive skin varieties and
special varieties for face and lips. You will probably need
several different types of these products when shelling in
summer months or at locations in the lower latitudes.

Items needed for convenience include a beach bag,
back pack, road atlas, hotel confirmation information, an
extra set of car keys, binoculars, and a travel/shelling log
book. It is helpful and enjoyable to record your travels
and experiences. You will remember the restaurants and

CHECK LIST OF ESSENTIAL ITEMS

COMFORT AND SAFETY ITEMS

_____hats   _____bug repellant
_____flash light   _____cooler
_____sweatshirts   _____beach umbrella
_____jackets   _____first aid kit
_____rain gear   _____sunscreen lotions
_____aqua-shoes/old sneakers
_____a well-supplied tool box
_____UV blocking sunglasses

SHELLING ITEMS

_____pail   _____tissues or paper towels
_____scoops   _____gallon size self-seal bags
_____plastic containers   _____shell identification books

CONVENIENCE ITEMS

_____beach bag   _____extra set of car keys
_____back packs   _____binoculars
_____road atlas   _____travel log book
_____accommodation confirmation information

SUPPLIES FOR FOUR-WHEELING IN YOUR OFF-ROAD VEHICLE

_____shovel   _____vehicle jack
_____jack support boards   _____tire gauge
_____tow rope

table 2   Check List of Essential Items

beaches you liked and hope to return to, and the ones to avoid. You will also have the facts about where you found shells and what techniques worked in specific areas.

There are other items needed specifically for shelling. They include a pail, gallon size heavy plastic self-seal bags, tissues or paper towels for packing fragile shells, scoops, plastic containers and shell identification books.

Precautions

Knowing what precautions to take can help make your shelling trip a safe one. Avoid injuries by making safety a habit. Also, be attentive to your personal security and the security of your belongings.

At beaches where you are required to have an off-road vehicle permit, you will probably receive an informational guide. Requirements will be similar to the following: while driving on the sand you must lower your tire pressure to 15 pounds per square inch (PSI); you must have a minimum tire width of eight inches; you must carry a shovel, vehicle jack and support board, tire gauge, and tow rope. Tips for safe off-road operation include: wear your seat belt, drive no faster than ten miles per hour, try to drive in the tire tracks of other vehicles, do not make sharp turns, stay to the dry side of the shell line and never drive in salt water. Salt water will definitely damage your vehicle. Also, be on the lookout for soft sand, uneven beach terrain, driftwood, and other vehicles. It is your responsibility to know and abide by the regulations of the area you are visiting. Regulations exist to help insure everyone's safe enjoyment of the fragile beach resources.

Always practice "sun safety." In Virginia, the Carolinas, and Florida, the sun is more intense than in the northern states.   Visitors to these southern states, un-accustomed to the strong subtropical sun, must be particularly aware of possible serious sunburn and dehydration.   To avoid heat-related illnesses, limit your exposure to the sun and avoid strenuous activities.   Avoid dehydration by drinking plenty of water.   Always use sun-screen lotions and wear light colored loose fitting clothes, UV blocking sunglasses, and a hat.   Watch for heat exhaustion symptoms–pale ashy-gray skin, heavy sweating, clammy skin, headache, nausea, weakness, dizziness, and muscle cramps.   More serious are heat stroke symptoms–skin blazing hot and dry, dazed and unresponsive reactions, fainting and/or convulsions.   In both cases cool the individual.   With heat stroke, immediately seek medical attention.

Another precaution is to avoid animals capable of stinging, pinching, or biting.   Some harmful creatures are very small, others quite large.   Crabs are residents of all the areas covered in this book.   The best way to avoid crab pinches is to wear sneakers or aqua-shoes.   You will not feel the pinches of most crabs through them.   Some urchins can be harmful too.   Their spines contain barbs with toxins.   If grabbed or stepped on, the urchin's spines can penetrate your skin and break off.   This can result in intense irritation.

Other animals to be careful of are stinging creatures. The Portuguese Man-of-War is one of the most dangerous stinging creatures in southern waters.   These animals have a blue balloon-like body keeping them afloat, enabling them to be propelled by the wind.   Attached to their bodies are stinging tentacles trailing through the water.   The tentacles of the larger Man-of-War may trail up to sixty feet.   Man-of-War can also be very small, sometimes barely noticeable. The sting of a Man-of-War can cause severe pain and even death. If you see one on the beach or in the water, stay away.

In some southern states you will see signs, "Do Not Feed the Alligators." They mean it. The signs are not displayed to create an atmosphere of excitement for tourists. When alligators are fed, they associate people with food. They then will approach people expecting to get fed. You do not want to be dinner. Anytime you see alligators, keep your distance. In a split second, they can get up and run at great speeds. You could not get out of the way if one wanted you.

Always be prepared for insects, especially mosquitoes, by packing bug repellant. Some people are more sensitive to mosquito bites than other people. However, everyone should avoid mosquitoes because they have the potential for spreading disease.

Since shelling is done in and around water, the following water safety tips should be observed: learn to swim, never shell hunt in the water alone when either walking or snorkeling, check with lifeguards regarding water conditions, and obey posted signs alerting you to dangerous conditions. Should you get caught in a rip current (they flow out to sea,) relax and swim parallel to the shoreline in the same direction as the current. Then, when you no longer feel the rip current, swim toward shore. Should other people be around, call or wave for help.

Wherever you travel, lock the car doors while driving. When you are away from your vehicle, keep it locked. Secure any valuables in the trunk. However, keep your car keys, hotel keys, wallet, and money with you. A small hip pack is a great way to carry these items. You can keep the hip pack zipped closed and walk relaxed while shelling. If you have your beach sundries in a bag on the beach, do not keep anything important in the bag. Unfortunately, there are individuals looking for any opportunity to steal. On one trip, we were planning to go snorkeling. It appeared we were the only people on the secluded beach. As we enjoyed the views and prepared to snorkel, we noticed someone peering through the bushes from a nearby hill. We were cautious and did not leave our belongings unattended. At dinner, a couple said someone on a nearby beach had their bag stolen when they were snorkeling. If we had not been careful, it could have been our experience also. It would be nice if these things did not happen; however, they do, so be cautious.

When you plan to have a good time, respect the regulations of the area you are visiting, and prepare for the expected and unexpected, you set the stage for having a safe and enjoyable shelling trip.

PART TWO:
SHELLING DESTINATIONS

4

Florida

Florida is one of the most popular vacation locations in the world, offering visitors a year-round warm and sunny climate. With sandy beaches, lakes, rivers, wildlife refuges, historic sites, and a variety of resorts and tourist attractions, there are geographic locations and activities to please everyone. For nature lovers, especially those who like to be on, in, or near the water, Florida is an ideal getaway. A peninsula with the Atlantic Ocean to its east and the Gulf of Mexico to its west, Florida is dotted with lakes and traversed with rivers and streams. Its southern tip includes the famous Everglades and Keys. With all this water, Florida offers many excellent shelling opportunities.

We have personally identified four different shelling regions in the state. They are the West Coast, the Florida Keys, the East Coast, and the inland areas. These regions are clearly distinguishable by the types of shells found in each area. As discussed in chapter one, different shell species live in different habitats. The four regions are environmentally dissimilar, resulting in different varieties of shells found in each. However, there is some overlap, as many mollusks can live in more than one region and currents often carry many shells from one region to another.

Shelling on the West Coast

Two excellent shelling spots on the West Coast are Honeymoon Island State Recreation Area, Dunedin, and world famous Sanibel Island. Many varieties of shell species can be found at these locations. Also on the West Coast is Venice, a popular destination for those who enjoy collecting fossilized sharks' teeth.

Sand Dollars at Honeymoon Island State Recreation Area

Honeymoon Island State Recreation Area, Dunedin, is located just north of Clearwater. Traveling on Route 19, take Route 586 west over the Dunedin Causeway and follow the road into the park.

Honeymoon Island is a barrier island approximately 7,000 years old. The first inhabitants of the island were the Tocobaga tribe. From the period 1530 to 1550, visitors included Spanish explorers, pirates, traders, and fishermen. In the 1830s the island was named Sand Island, and when later used for hog farming renamed Hog Island. In the early 1940s and until Pearl Harbor, the Island was a honeymoon resort for newlyweds. During World War II, the island was recommissioned as a getaway spot for factory workers. In 1964 a causeway was completed between the island and the mainland, leading builders to attempt developing the island. Fortunately, in 1974 the Department of

Natural Resources acquired the undeveloped acres of Honeymoon Island and established this coastal recreational area. Along with great shelling, visitors can enjoy bird watching, picnicking, hiking, swimming, sunbathing, and fishing. Please note, taking live shells from Honeymoon Island State Recreation Area is not allowed.

Shells Commonly Found on Honeymoon Island:

Keyhole Urchin	Cross-barred Venus
Lettered Olive	Chestnut Turban
Florida Cone	Common American Auger
True Tulip	Florida Fighting Conch
Turkey Wing	Common Jingle Shell
Sunray Venus	Long-spined Urchin
Lightning Whelk	

Upon entering the park be sure to ask for a brochure. Proceed to the last parking area on the gulf beach side of the island (map 1.) Park here and walk north, up the beach, to Sand Spit. The walk to Sand Spit is about two miles. It will take almost an hour to get to the best shelling spot, so be prepared and bring all needed supplies, including drinking water.

At the beginning of the walk, just past the restrooms and changing facilities, the beach will be very rocky. Wearing shoes or sneakers on this part of the walk is highly recommended. The rocks are very interesting; examine them closely. They are made of limestone and contain shell and plant fossils. Fossils are naturally buried and preserved remains or imprints of organisms from past geologic ages. The white chalk-like rocks at Honeymoon Island State Recreation Area con-

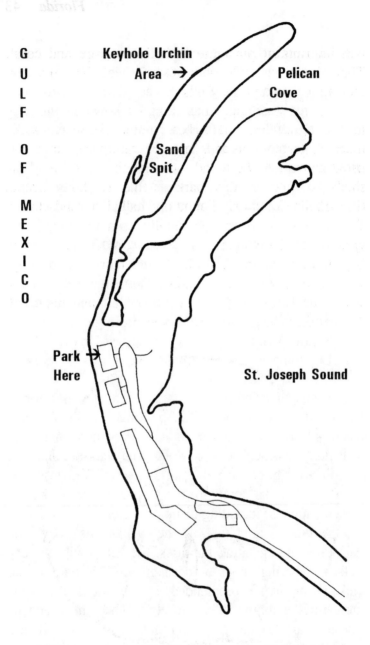

map 1 Honeymoon Island State Recreation Area, Florida

tain imprints of plant life including sponge and coral. They also contain a variety of shells and shell imprints, including snail and ark shells.

After examining the fossils, continue walking toward Sand Spit. The beach soon becomes sandy, much easier to walk on, and several species of shells listed above may be found. One of the most enjoyable shells to find at this park is the Keyhole Urchin (illustration 3,) more commonly called a sand dollar. The term sand dollar is generally used to describe all varieties of flat circular sea urchins. A Keyhole Urchin is identified by the keyhole-shaped holes in its body. The Keyhole Urchins commonly found here range from silver dollar size to about six inches in diameter, with the majority being three to five inches.

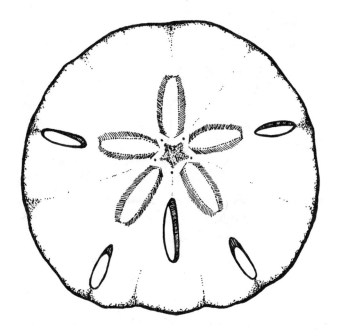

illustration 3 Keyhole Urchin

Keyhole Urchins, like other sea urchins, are bottom dwellers unable to swim. These animals live just under the surface of the sand. They use hundreds of minute tube-like feet or velvety fine spines on their underside to move along the sandy ocean or bay floor. Keyhole Urchins are disk-shaped, of radial symmetry having a spoke-like arrangement of five petal-like designs radiating from a central point. These animals' skeletons, called tests, act as a protective shell. When they are alive, Keyhole Urchins have a greenish spiny skin. When they die the spines fall off, the shells wash around in the surf, and they are then bleached white by the sun.

Continue walking toward Sand Spit. You will begin to see more and more pieces of Keyhole Urchins, with an occasional whole one being found. Do not linger here. The area of the park most productive for finding urchins is about 1/4 mile from the end of Sand Spit, on the gulf side. As you walk, keep looking toward Pelican Cove until you notice another peninsula covered with a stand of trees. When standing opposite the end of this peninsula, you are at the best spot for finding Keyhole Urchins.

The hunt for Keyhole Urchins should be a rewarding one if you arrive at this location an hour or so before low tide. At low tide a sandbar is visible just off the beach. Wade out to the sandbar. The water should be knee to thigh deep, depending on the tide. The sandbar catches urchins before they wash onto shore. Keyhole Urchins found on the sandbar range in size from four to six inches in diameter and are usually a brown or greenish color. See the chapter "Caring for Your Shells" to learn how to bleach Keyhole Urchins.

It is not necessary to go out to the sandbar to find urchins. They can also be found on the beach. Keyhole Urchins found on the beach are generally smaller than those found on the sandbar and many have been bleached white by the sun. They range in size from one and one-half to four inches in diameter. Patience and a sharp eye are required for discovering urchins uncovered by the gentle back and forth movement of the water as small waves break onto shore. In drier sand, keen observation will enable you to see the center of the urchin crowning the surface. Very carefully scrape the sand out from around the urchin. Gently dig under the sand and under the urchin, lifting both the sand and the urchin up together. Urchins are fragile, so do this slowly. Once the urchin is out of the sand, wash it off and admire your beautiful find. The best method for carrying urchins safely is to stack them flat in a plastic pail. Be careful not to place Keyhole Urchins and shells together or the urchins will break.

Before heading back, be sure to walk to the very end of Sand Spit and enjoy the beautiful view. From here it will take about an hour to walk back, so avoid getting too hot or tired.

Sanibel Island: Shells, Shells, and More Shells

Sanibel Island is considered by many to be among the top ten best shelling locations in the world. It is also considered to be the best shelling location in the Western Hemisphere. There are about 275 species of mollusks found in the shallow waters of Sanibel. Five hundred more species live offshore in 80 to 2,000 feet of water. Additionally, almost a thousand species of mollusks represented by a billion shells, live along an 80 mile wide continental shelf. This shelf extends a thousand miles from Alabama to the lower Florida Keys.

Sanibel is located about twenty-three miles west of Fort Meyers. To get to Sanibel Island and its neighbor Captiva Island, exit Route 75 at exit 21, heading west to State Highway 869. Turn left onto the Sanibel Causeway. There is a bridge toll to get onto the island. After crossing the causeway, look to your right for the Sanibel-Captiva Islands Chamber of Commerce building. Stop here for information about the area and for detailed beach access maps.

On Sanibel's beaches, at the high water line, there is a band of mostly worn and broken shells of many different species. When walking along the water's edge, you can hear and feel buried shells crunching under foot. Also, listen for the chiming of shells as they move back and forth with every wave. Up and down the beach, literally for as far as the eye can see, there will be hundreds of shellers and beach strollers. The people shell hunting are easy to spot by their bent over posture referred to as the "Sanibel stoop."

Keep in mind all shell hunting locations, including Sanibel Island, have better shelling days than others. There have been times when we were happy to find a gallon size bag of "keepers" after shelling for eight hours. Yet on other days, especially after a storm, the number and varieties of shells made for a shell hunter's "dream come true." Typically, December, January, and February are the best shelling months. One February morning, a storm passed through and the air temperature dropped from the low 70's to 34 degrees. The strong wind pushed the water out about 150 feet farther than usual. The shelling was terrific!

Sanibel juts out into the Gulf of Mexico in a westerly direction and catches the shells pushed northward by the prevailing winds and currents. In winter the surface water is pushed away from the land when cold winds from the north or northwest blow across the island. Bottom currents flow in the direction of the land to replace the surface waters. This wind and current action uproots shells and brings them ashore in great numbers. In the summer and early fall, mild surface currents pile up against Sanibel Island. The extra water retreats in the form of bottom currents, taking beach shells and sand back out to sea. Sometimes violent summer thunderstorms from the north reverse this cycle.

Often there will be two lines of debris on the beach. Mixed in with the shells you will see other sea life including Purple Sea Urchins, sea squirts, and Parchment Worms. You will probably see a lot of pen shells on the beach, too. Although brown and considered unattractive on the outside, these quill pen-shaped shells have a beautiful pearly layer on the inside.

Occasionally shells on the beach can be seen moving. After an extremely high tide or during an unusually low tide, many live mollusks and shells occupied by hermit crabs are left stranded on the beach. While waiting for a life saving high tide, the hermit crabs will curl up deep inside their found homes. Florida Fighting Conch, Apple Murex (illustration 4,) and others will thrash about if upside down as they attempt to turn over to keep from drying out. Stranded mollusks can live out of water for about twenty-four hours.

The inner bays of Sanibel Island are protected from the open ocean by barrier islands and shallow basins.

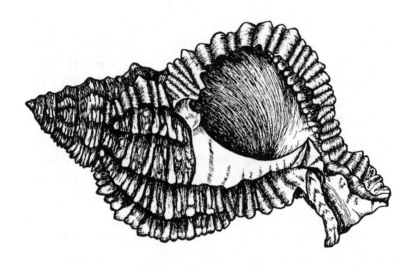

illustration 4 Apple Murex

The mangrove trees, marine grasses, and mud bottoms of the bays offer habitats for oysters, tulip shells, Southern Quahogs, and Angel Wings. Natural occurrences such as long droughts, heavy rains, and hot and cold weather can make the mollusks' existence difficult. The variations in temperature, salinity, and water clarity limit the species of shells that can survive in this environment.

When shelling on Sanibel Island remember their shell law–NO LIVE SHELLING! In 1995, the state of Florida passed a law declaring it illegal to collect live shells on Sanibel Island. This law became necessary as a result of the increased popularity of shelling on the island, possibly contributing to the depletion of shell populations. The taking of live sand dollars, sea stars, and sea urchins is also prohibited.   All shelling is prohibited in J.N. "Ding" Darling Refuge.   Captiva Island follows the county law and restricts the taking of live shells to two species per person per day.   We advocate "no live shelling" anywhere.   A serious threat to mollusks is habitat destruction.   Silt runoff and man made pollution destroy habitat.

Shellers are also urged to limit their non-live shell collecting to shells they know they will use and admire. Empty shells on the beach help to build the beach by collecting the blowing sand.   This is much better than empty shells collecting dust in your basement.

The most sought after shell on Sanibel is the Junonia (illustration 5.)   A univalve, it belongs to the volute family.   It is an elongated spiral shell and grows to four and one-half inches.   It is white or yellowish

illustration 5 Junonia

white with spiral rows of square-shaped brown spots.
The animal that inhabits the shell is colored the same as
its shell. The Junonia's spots resemble the spots on a
peacock's tail feathers. The peacock was known to
ancients as the "bird of Juno" resulting in the shell's
name, Junonia. Unlike many other univalves, the
Junonia does not have an operculum. Although the
shell's range is from North Carolina to both coasts of
Florida, it is a rare find because it lives in water from 40
to 250 feet deep.

Shells Commonly Found on Sanibel Island:

Banded Tulip (illustration 6)	Common Fig Shell
True Tulip	Pear Whelk
Lightning Whelk	Alphabet Cone
Measled Cowry	Turkey Wing
Atlantic Yellow Cowry	Channeled Whelk
Florida Fighting Conch	Florida Cone
Common Nutmeg	Calico Scallop
Atlantic Hair Triton	Lettered Olive
Florida Lace Murex	Stiff Pen Shell
Saw-toothed Pen Shell	Adele's Top Shell
Say's False Limpet	Apple Murex
Florida Crown Conch	Ponderous Ark
West Indian Worm Shell	Florida Cerith
Florida Spiny Jewel Box	
Sunray Venus (illustration 7)	
Florida Horse Conch (illustration 8, State Shell)	

Shells can be found on all of Sanibel's beaches.
Our favorite shelling spots are the beaches along East
Gulf and Middle Gulf Drives on the south end of the
island. Sanibel residents also boast about the shelling on

illustration 6 Banded Tulip

the beach off Algiers Lane and on Bowman's Beach. In these areas the offshore sandy bottom is shallow and gently sloped. This slope allows many shells to roll up onto the beach unbroken. The shelling technique used by most people on Sanibel is beach strolling. It is important to look closely in the many piles of shell pieces. Sort through these piles to find the whole shells missed by others. However, the best shelling is in the subtidal zone, especially when there are crowds of people on the beach. Here a productive method is to wade in the water and scoop up the shells either with your hands, a net, or a sieve.

Another good shelling spot is at Blind Pass, between Sanibel and Captiva Islands. To get there take Sanibel-Captiva Road and park at the bridge. Beginning in 1911, a county ferry was used to cross the pass.   In 1918 the first Blind Pass bridge was built.   Then in the 1980's a new bridge was built capable of withstanding the rushing water in the narrow pass.   There are public beaches on either side of the bridge.   We suggest walking under the bridge on the Sanibel Island side. Here you can look for shells on the gulf beach or inside the pass.   Low tide will allow you to wade to a sandbar between the islands and shell collect with only a few other people.   On occasion, usually after a storm, the pass will fill in with sand and shells only to open again after another storm.

While shelling, take the time to examine the sand. It is white with very few particles of other colors.   The composition of the sand is very fine granules of white sun bleached shell pieces and crushed coral.

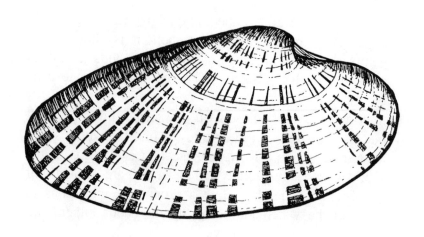

illustration 7 Sunray Venus

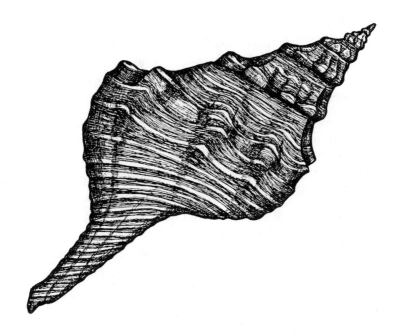

illustration 8 Florida Horse Conch

Years of pulverizing wave action have created sand with
a texture finer than the consistency of sugar. It is very
soft to walk on.

   In addition to shelling, Sanibel Island offers many
other activities. A fun and educational adventure for
shell lovers is the Bailey-Matthews Shell Museum
located on Sanibel-Captiva Road.   The museum is
devoted entirely to seashells. There are many intriguing
displays exhibiting nearly a third of the world's total
shell specimens. You will delight at the visual presen-
tation. Special exhibits include Mollusks, Medicine and
Man, Gifts From the Seas of Sanibel & Captiva,
Kingdom of the Land Shells, Shells in Tribal Art,
Southwest Florida Fossil Shells, and The Scallop. The
exhibits contain habitat panoramas, explain the biology

of shells, show the history of Florida fossils, and tell how shells are a part of our history and lives. If you did not find the shells you were looking for on the beach, you will find them in the Bailey-Matthews Shell Museum.

Not to be missed is J.N. "Ding" Darling National Wildlife Refuge. This wildlife refuge is named after the late Pulitzer Prize winning conservationist, cartoonist, and Captiva resident. The 5,014 acre refuge helps to preserve the mangroves and wetlands forming the bayside shore of Sanibel Island. Here, walk, ride a bicycle, or drive along a five-mile dirt road and observe the wildlife. The refuge is inhabited or visited by 290 species of birds, fifty types of reptiles, and many mammals. Turtles, alligators, raccoons, white pelicans, roseate spoonbills, ospreys, egrets, and herons are likely to be seen here.

Sanibel offers a twenty-mile system of well-maintained bike trails traversing through residential areas and along main thoroughfares. The trails help to get you all around the Island. Biking gives you the opportunity to enjoy more of the nature you came to see while avoiding congested roadways.

Venice, "The Shark Tooth Mecca of the World"

Venice, often referred to as "The Shark Tooth Mecca of the World," is located on the Gulf of Mexico approximately eighteen miles south of Sarasota and seventy-one miles south of Tampa. Traveling south on Route 75 take exit 36 and travel south on Route 681 to Route 41 southbound. Traveling north on Route 75, exit at Route 33, head west, and pick up Route 41 north to Venice. There is a small airport located walking distance from the Venice Fishing Pier should a small plane be your mode of transportation.

Venice has several public beaches with restrooms and changing facilities. The best section of beach for collecting sharks' teeth is from just north of the fishing pier, located on Harbor Drive adjacent the airport, to the south end of Caspersen Beach. The beach is long and narrow. In many areas the sand is very black because of a high concentration of fossil particles.

Sharks have many rows of teeth waiting to replace the teeth they are using. Some species of shark can produce up to 20,000 teeth in their lifetime. For millions of years sharks have lived and died in the Gulf of Mexico. After the sharks died and their bodies decayed, the teeth became buried in the sandy bottom. The teeth absorbed minerals from the sand and silt and turned brown, black, or gray, depending on the color of the minerals they were buried in. Sharks' teeth (illustration 9) found on the beaches of Venice are millions of

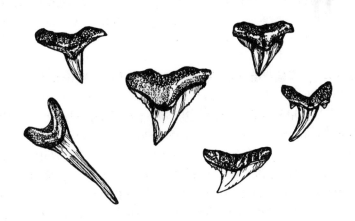

illustration 9   Sharks' Teeth

years old. Every species of shark has distinctly different shaped teeth, making identification easy. Sharks' teeth range in size from one-eighth inch to three or more inches, with larger sizes being rare. In addition to finding sharks' teeth, you will find pieces of ray mouth plates. Finding a one-eighth inch shark's tooth on a sandy beach is not as difficult as one would imagine. Most of the teeth found here are this size to about one inch.

The following methods can be used successfully to find sharks' teeth. At low tide, search the area of the beach being washed over by the waves. As the water retreats, look for one or two teeth sliding down the beach in the wet sand. Move quickly to pick them up before the next wave washes over the sand and covers them. An hour of intense searching should result in a handful of sharks' teeth.

Another method, at any tide, is to use a specially made sieve-like scoop. Rent a scoop at the pier or purchase one at a hardware store in town. Take the scoop to the water's edge and walk into about ankle- to knee-deep water. Look for areas where pieces of shells and stones have gathered and scoop about an inch or two deep into the sand. Then lift the scoop and shake it gently in the water to remove most of the sand. Walk up onto the beach and carefully sort through what remains in the scoop. There will probably be mole crabs, pieces of shells, some whole shells, sand, and usually mouth plates from rays. Continue sifting the material while looking into the scoop. As you sift, sharks' teeth will appear. When you think you have found all the sharks' teeth in the scoop, dump the rest of the material onto the beach above the water line and continue looking. You will usually find more. In some scoops there will be several teeth and in other scoops none. Often you can find them by reexamining what other people have scooped up, searched through, and left behind on the beach. Also, observe others as they look for sharks' teeth. It's a great way to learn some "tricks of the trade."

Shelling in the Florida Keys

The Florida Keys, located at the southernmost tip of Florida, are 110 miles of small islands connected by the bridges of Highway US 1. The Keys begin at Key Largo and end at Key West with Marathon being approximately halfway between.

The majority of the ride down the Keys provides magnificent views of beautiful blue, turquoise, and green water. The extremely clear water and lime from the coral reefs are two major reasons for all this color. In the Florida Keys, along with water, you'll be surrounded by tropical weather, lush vegetation, beautiful birds, and coral reefs. It is truly Caribbean-like.

There are many enjoyable things to do when visiting the Keys. You can rent a boat and go sight seeing, go deep sea or bay fishing, go snorkeling at the coral reefs, spend a day shopping at Key West, or just hang out and relax at the beach. But, no matter what you do all day, take the time to enjoy the spectacular sunsets.

Yes, there are beaches in the Keys, although many times people say otherwise. Actually, there are several beautiful public beaches tucked away in the "nooks and crannies" of the Keys. Characteristically, the beaches are narrow with alternating coral rock shoreline and sandy beach. Favorite beaches are, from north to south,

Long Key State Recreation Area, mile marker 67.5 (MM 67.5), Sombrero Beach (MM 50), and Bahia Honda State Recreation Area (MM 36.5.)

A Sampling of Shells Represented Throughout the Keys:

Angular Triton	Measled Cowry
Bleeding Tooth Nerite	Caribbean Vase
Common American Auger	Four-toothed Nerite
Caribbean False Cerith	Ivory Cerith
Common Purple Snail	Dwarf Cerith
Common Dove Shell	Cabrit's Murex
Well-ribbed Dove Shell	Pink Conch
Orange Margin Shell	Say's False Limpet
Long-spined Star Shell	Jasper Cone
Sculptured Top Shell	Jasper Dwarf Olive
West Indian Worm Shell	Netted Olive
Common Atlantic Bubble	

Florida shells come from two different zones–the Caribbean Marine Faunal Province and the Carolinian Province. These two zones overlap in south Florida. As a result, shelling in south Florida can net many varieties of shells. When shelling in the Keys, be aware that most areas are off limits to live shelling.

Miniature Shells at Sombrero Beach

An excellent spot for shelling is Sombrero Beach, Marathon. Heading south on US 1 at MM 50, make a left turn onto Sombrero Beach Road and follow it all the way to the end. Watch the speed bumps! Here you will find a beautiful serene beach. Take a deep breath of fresh air and enjoy the soothing view.

The "residents" of Sombrero Beach include great white herons, great blue herons, and brown pelicans. In recent years the endangered burrowing owl has made its home here. And always be on the lookout for a passing flamingo or even a manatee enjoying a leisurely swim. This free beach offers picnic areas, a roped-in swimming section, and restrooms.

Shelling here is easy. Simply walk along the water's edge, stoop down, and you will see miniature shells scattered along the edge of the wash. One morning we were crawling along the water's edge shelling when we sensed "someone" walking immediately behind us. As we turned to greet our fellow sheller, much to our surprise we had been joined by a great blue heron. To the heron, we probably looked like we were feeding, as we were plucking up our find like a heron catching its breakfast.

Shells found at Sombrero Beach are very small. These miniature shells are adult shells less than one inch in length. The larger miniature shells are one-half to one inch in size and can be found all along the water's edge. However, the most productive shelling areas are near the coral ledges and at the beach area near the canal.

To find even smaller miniature shells, scoop up a handful of sand and look at it closely. A magnifying glass will be helpful. The sand appears very white, but looking at it closely will reveal particles of brown, red, and green. Little pieces of coral, urchin spines, small pieces of shells, and very small whole shells make up the sand. Amazingly, you will see minute whole shells from one-eighth inch to less than one-sixteenth inch. Notice the sand feels different from most other beach sand. Light and very fine, not granular, it will stick to your feet and not brush off easily.

Spirula shells are another interesting find on Sombrero Beach. These small coiled shells look like miniature rams' horns. Instead of being a mollusk's external support, these shells from small deep-sea squid are internal supports. When the squid dies and decomposes, the spirula shells float to the surface and wash ashore.

A few hours of leisurely shelling at Sombrero will produce a couple of handfuls of shells. When you get home, put them in small decorative glass jars. They make beautiful souvenirs and interesting conversation pieces. Then every time you examine these miniature treasures, you will be transported back to beautiful Sombrero Beach.

Bahia Honda and Long Key State Recreation Areas, The "Original Natural Florida"

Florida's state parks represent the "original natural Florida." They are managed and maintained to appear as they did when the first Europeans arrived. Two parks having similar natural environments are Bahia Honda State Recreation Area, located just south of the Seven Mile Bridge at MM 36.5, and Long Key State Recreation Area located on Long Key at MM 67.5. These parks are ancient coral reefs now covered by beach, dunes, mangroves, and coastal stand hammocks and have a number of plants not often found on the other islands. The seeds of these tropical plants were brought to the islands from the West Indies by birds, ocean currents, and winds. Spiny catesbaea, satinwood tree, and dwarf morning glory are some rarer species of plants at Bahia Honda State Recreation Area. Species of trees and shrubs found at Long Key State Recreation Area include mahogany, gumbo limbo, Jamaica dogwood, poisonwood, and crabwood.

Shelling on the beaches of Bahia Honda and Long Key State Recreation Areas is quite different from shelling at Sombrero Beach. Here, beach collectibles such as sponge, sea fans, and other plant life can be found washed up onto the beach and coral mounds.

One good area for shelling at Bahia Honda is on Sandspar Beach near the camping area. After paying an entrance fee at the ranger station, proceed to the stop sign and then make a left turn. Follow this road to the first parking area located immediately past the campground and park here. Once on the beach turn right and walk toward the campground. Make this a leisurely stroll, turning over and searching through all the driftwood and sea grass, being very careful of the often present Portuguese Man-of-War. As you continue your walk, keep looking for old coral reefs exposed at the water's edge. Remember to plan your shell hunting to take advantage of the outgoing tide. All around the old reefs and in the trapped pools of water will be the best shelling. In this area it is very important to protect your feet from the sharp coral and vegetation.

As always be aware of local regulations and respect the natural environment. Park regulations prohibit the collection of Pink Conch, also called Queen Conch, and live shells.

Snorkeling at John Pennekamp Coral Reef State Park

Snorkeling is a method used to observe mollusks and other species of marine animals in their natural underwater environment. You can snorkel on your own off a beach, take a private snorkeling tour, rent a boat and locate your own spot, or take a guided tour at John Pennekamp Coral Reef State Park.

John Pennekamp Coral Reef State Park is the first underwater state park in the United States. It is located at mile marker 102.5, north of Key Largo. The park is named after the late John Pennekamp, a Miami newspaper editor. He contributed to the establishment of the Everglades National Park and to the continuation and conservation of Florida's State Park System. John Pennecamp Park contains approximately 53,593 acres of submerged land. It extends almost three miles into the ocean and is about twenty-five miles in length. Skeletal remains of corals, living coral, and other plants and animals make up the coral reefs within the park. Many species of marine animals and mollusks live in this habitat.

Rangers provide special snorkeling programs to familiarize park visitors and first time snorkelers with this method of observing the reefs. Snorkeling boat tours are provided daily, weather permitting. You may bring your own equipment or rent it in the park. While snorkeling, never touch or stand on the coral reefs. They are fragile and this will kill living coral.

Shelling on the East Coast

A very good shelling location on the East Coast of Florida is John U. Lloyd Beach State Recreation Area,

Dania. Shell collecting is also enjoyable at Canaveral National Seashore/Merrit Island National Wildlife Refuge. The shelling environment of the East Coast of Florida is quite different from the West Coast of Florida. The Atlantic Ocean has greater wave action than the Gulf of Mexico resulting in fewer whole shells washing onto the beach. The water on the East Coast is deeper closer to shore and is home to deep water shell species not found on the West Coast.

Deep Water Scallops at John U. Lloyd Beach State Recreation Area

John U. Lloyd Beach State Recreation Area is located in Dania, off A1A. This is a 251 acre state park consisting of dunes, coastal hammocks, and mangroves. The environment at John U. Lloyd State Recreation Area greatly contrasts the nearby urban developments. At this park, fishing, canoeing, swimming, and picnicking can be enjoyed. A boat ramp is available near the Port Everglades Inlet for access to the protected Intracoastal Waterway or Atlantic Ocean.

The beach at John U. Lloyd Beach State Recreation Area is long and can be enjoyed without the interruption of rock jetties or coral mounds. We recommend driving to the northern-most parking area near the jetty boardwalk. Beach strolling is the most productive shelling technique to use here. You will find many shells on the beach and in the shallow water among the rocks.

The shells found here include deep water shell species such as the Lion's Paw and Kitten's Paw. Colorful scallops such as the Zigzag Scallop and the Calico Scallop are also good finds at this park.

Sampling of Shells Found at
John U. Lloyd Beach State Recreation Area:

Kitten's Paw	Frons Oyster
Florida Spiny Jewel Box	Lion's Paw
Atlantic Thorny Oyster	Florida Cone
Common Egg Cockle	Zigzag Scallop
West Indian Worm Shell	Sentis Scallop
Atlantic Wing Oyster	Hawk-wing Conch
Atlantic Rough File Shell	Atlantic Bittersweet
Calico Scallop (illustration 10)	

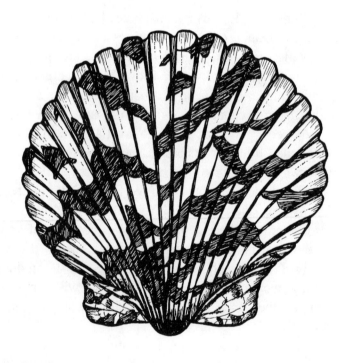

illustration 10   Calico Scallop

Scallop shells are very attractive, consisting of many colors with endless pattern combinations. It is fun to find the different species and different colors. Scallops are used for decorative displaying and craft projects as they add design and color. The assortment of colors includes white, black, and shades of gray, tan, orange, pink, and burgundy. One half of the scallop's shell is usually darker than the other half. Beautiful Sentis Scallops come in a variety of brilliant shades of orange and yellow. Scallop shells are basically circular with one valve usually more convex than the other. The protruding wing-like triangular extensions are a feature unique to the scallop. They are called ears. The flat edge along the ears is the hinge area. When shelling, you rarely find the valves attached. Most scallops have radial ribs or ridges meeting at a central point at the hinge. The most popular scallops are the bay and the Calico Scallops. Bay scallops live in bays; they are swept out into the ocean by the movement of tides and often wash up onto the ocean beaches. The bay scallop is the most desirable to eat, but Calico Scallops are more abundant and are usually the scallops served in restaurants.

Angel Wings at Canaveral National Seashore/Merritt Island National Wildlife Refuge

Canaveral National Seashore and Merritt Island National Wildlife Refuge are located northeast of Orlando and immediately north of Cape Canaveral. Traveling on Route 1 or Interstate 95, take Route 406 east at Titusville. After going over the Indian River, take Route 402 east to the Merritt Island National Wildlife Refuge Visitor Information Center. Stop at the visitor center and pick up brochures for the seashore and wildlife refuge.   A U.S. Fish and Wildlife Service Volunteer will provide information about the area and answer any questions you may have. Be sure to ask the refuge volunteer where to find the manatee. They can often be seen playing in small lagoons. Around these lagoons the opportunity exists to photograph live mollusks, including True Tulips. Also ask about Black Point Wildlife Drive, an excellent educational tour of the salt marsh and its inhabitants.

This national seashore is a barrier island and has about twenty-one miles of beach. The beach here is long and narrow.   At times, with the right combination of onshore wind, rough surf, and high tide, there may be little beach to walk on. Although there may not be an abundance of shell species found here, your shelling experience will be enhanced by the many large Angel Wings (illustration 11) usually scattered on the beach.

The Most Commonly Found Shells Along
Canaveral's Shores:

Prickly Cockle	Angel Wing
Stiff Pen Shell	Green Jackknife Clam
Calico Scallop	Lightning Whelk
Shark Eye	White Miniature Ark
Coquina Shell	Eastern Oyster

Angel Wings vary in size from four to eight inches in length. The average size is about five inches.   Their habitat is in deep, soft, sandy mud at or just below low-tide level to water 60 feet deep.   Their range is from southern Massachusetts to the northern West Indies, Texas, and Brazil. The shells are delicate and easily

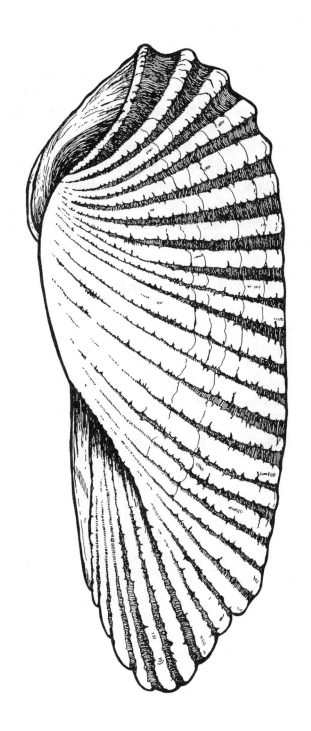

illustration 11   Angel Wing

break in the surf, but with persistence several large whole ones can be found.   Angel Wings are elongated oval-shaped bivalves with ribs radiating from the hinge area.   The shells of most Angel Wings are white.   Rarer Angel Wing shells have a ribbon of pink in the inside.

Another possible find at Canaveral is the "Crucifix." This is not a shell, but a bone from the skull of a catfish. It is white, intricate in design and, as the name implies, it resembles Christ on the Cross–an interesting, unusual, and rare find.

Shelling Inland

Inland Florida offers two types of shelling. Shells from fresh water mollusks can be found in and around the rivers and lakes.   Fossil shells from a salt water environment can be found throughout the interior as the whole of Florida was once covered by ocean.

Fresh Water Shelling at Lake Kissimmee

Lake Kissimmee encompasses approximately sixty-three square miles.   It is located in Osceola County about forty miles north-northwest of Lake Okeechobee.   The Kissimmee River flows out from this lake, south to Lake Okeechobee. An airboat ride on Lake Kissimmee allows access to wetlands without disturbing the ecosystem. This environmentally sensitive method of observing the wetlands provides the opportunity to see Florida wilderness.   Besides beautiful flora, interesting wildlife inhabits this area.   Alligators, otter, deer, armadillos, wild pigs, the American bald eagle, wood storks, red shouldered hawks, and the Everglade Kite are frequently seen.

While touring Lake Kissimmee, ask the airboat tour guide to point out the floating islands, called tussocks. When stopping next to one of these islands, look in the grassy areas for piles of Apple Snail shells. Do not reach for these shells as snakes and alligators may be lurking. Instead, ask the guide to get one or two shells for you. Apple Snails are fresh water snails approximately two inches in diameter, slightly bigger than a golf ball. In contrast to salt water snails, these snails have much thinner shells. The Everglade Kite, a hawk-like bird also called a "Snail Kite," feeds almost exclusively on Apple Snails. The kite's bill is slender, sharply hooked, and easily extracts the animal without breaking the shell.

Fossil Shells

Once, the ocean covered the Florida peninsula. As a result, fossil shells can be found in almost all areas of the state. These fossil deposits range in age from approximately 100,000 to 50 million years.

Mollusks were among the first of the primitive animal groups, dating back nearly 540 million years. One hundred million years later, all six classes of mollusks were in some primitive stage of development. To put this into perspective, dinosaurs roamed the earth as far back as only 65 million years ago.

Fossils are the preserved remains of dead plants and animals. They have become part of the earth's rocks and sediments. The term fossil is usually associated with bones, but any organism with a hard skeleton or shell can become a fossil after death. Animals, to include mollusks, die and become buried. Sand or mud surrounds the shell and hardens into rock.

Sometimes water seeps into the cavity and dissolves the shell.   Steinkerns are internal casts formed when mud fills a shell and hardens into rock.   When the shell eventually breaks away, the internal mold of the shell becomes exposed.   Internal features, such as the muscle scars of bivalves, are often visible on these molds.

Direct fossils are more than 20 million years old. The shells are unchanged except their colors have faded. The white, calcareous shells of the Pliocene beds of Florida are a typical example.   Practically all the organic parts, including the periostracum and the inner pigments are removed by time.

The value of fossils lies in the scientific information they contain.   They hold the clues used to determine how animals and plants evolved or when they became extinct.   Shell fossils are the ancestors of shell species that live today.

Our Florida fossil shelling experiences have been on private property east of Lake Wales.   Lake Wales is located in the center of the state, halfway between Vero Beach and Tampa.   We stumbled upon a bull pasture appearing to have been dug up and slightly overgrown again. Looking for fossil shells was easy because the shells were not buried, but strewn about on the surface. This is what initially attracted our attention to the area. After a couple hours of picking through the dirt, we were rewarded with a gallon size pail of fossil shells. All the shells were a whitish putty color.   The varieties of shells found included tusk, oyster, turret, mussel, cone, and several types of clam.   Some of the shells found resembled the Shark Eye, Common Rice Olive, Lettered Olive, Atlantic Partridge Tun, Imperial Venus, and Crested Oyster.   Evolutionary changes are very noticeable when comparing the fossil shells to shells found on beaches today.

Throughout the state, mining operations are taking place to dig out shells from ten to twenty feet below the surface. The shells are used as foundation material for parking lots, roads, and railroad beds. Most mining operations are on private property; it is important to receive permission before shelling in these areas.

The variety of shells and environments in Florida provides novice and experienced shellers numerous opportunities to expand their shelling knowledge and shell collections. In this chapter, the shelling locations discussed are not the only productive shell hunting areas in the state. There are many more areas to explore. Transferring the information presented in this book to other shelling destinations will help you have many successful shelling experiences.

5

Ocracoke Island, NC

North Carolina's Outer Banks is a chain of barrier islands located approximately one mile from the mainland at its closest point to about thirty miles at its farthest. This ribbon of sand is generally a few hundred yards to a mile wide. It is separated from the mainland by shallow bodies of water called sounds.

These barrier islands began to form approximately 10,000 years ago. The islands of sand seen today are estimated to be about 5,000 years old (Alexander and Lazell, 1992.) At the time of formation, the mainland extended approximately fifty miles out into the ocean. As glaciers melted, the sea level rose and water flowed over, around, and through the coastal dunes. This flooding of the coastal plains created the sounds. The glaciers continued to melt and the resulting water, laden with vast amounts of gravel, rock, and sand, emptied into the sounds and consequently built up the barrier islands. Thirty-five hundred years ago, another outflow of sand and sediments caused the barrier islands to grow. You would think the islands to be secure, fixed in place. However, as a result of winds, storms, and ocean currents, the Outer Banks is a geological system constantly moving westward.

The migration of sand is of interest to the shell collector. Every wave, gust of wind, and tide change, moves a tremendous amount of sand, covering and uncovering the shells you want to find. Putting sand movement into perspective, a wave 250 yards long can move about 1½ million pounds of sand, equaling about 24,000 cubic feet. The wave would weigh about 4,000 tons, consisting of about 140,000 cubic feet of water (Alexander and Lazell, 1992.)

Shelling on Ocracoke Island

Ocracoke Island encompasses 16 of the 180 miles of Outer Banks. Located at the southern end of Cape Hatteras National Seashore, it can be reached by car ferry, small plane, or boat.

Ocracoke consists of hammock woodlands, salt marshes, tidal flats, sand dunes, and sandy beaches. After getting off the ferry from Cape Hatteras and for the next fourteen miles, you will view scrub vegetation and the Pamlico Sound to your right. On your left will be beautiful sand dunes, covered with sea oats, overlooking the Atlantic Ocean. Four-fifths of the island is unspoiled wilderness owned and protected by the National Park Service. The village of Ocracoke is situated sound-side on the southern end of the island (map 2.)

When you drive through Ocracoke Village, a town of approximately 700 year-round residents, you see the

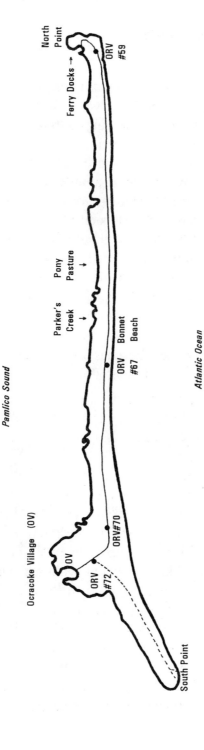

map 2 Ocracoke Island, North Carolina

homes of native Ocracokers, vacation cottages, hotels, restaurants, and gift shops. Silver Lake Harbor, in the center of town, is home to visiting sailboats, fishermen's work vessels, and large car ferries. When visiting here, it is very easy to put aside the cares of daily routine. You can relax by strolling around town, taking a leisurely bicycle ride, shopping, or just sitting on the porch of your cottage or hotel. Other enjoyable activities include fishing, surfing, sailboarding, kayaking, swimming, and bird watching. However, exploring the sixteen miles of beach while shelling will probably consume most of your time.

Shells can be found on all of Ocracoke's beaches. Traveling south on Route 12 from Hatteras Inlet to Ocracoke Inlet, the best beaches for shelling are North Point, Bonnet Beach, and South Point.

Shells commonly found on Ocracoke Island:

Keyhole Urchin	Shark Eye
Giant Atlantic Cockle	Ivory Tusk
Knobbed Whelk	Eared Ark
Reticulated Cowry Helmet	Disk Dosinia
Slipper Shell	Queen Helmet
Channeled Whelk	Scotch Bonnet
Lettered Olive	Coquina Shell
Lightning Whelk	Calico Scallop
White Bearded Ark	Turkey Wing
Common Jingle Shell	Ponderous Ark
Atlantic Razor Clam	Angel Wing
Northern Quahog	Atlantic Surf Clam
Crosshatched Lucine	
Common American Auger	
Common Atlantic Baby's Ear	

Olive Shells at North Point

North Point is located at Hatteras Inlet on the north end of Ocracoke Island. The best way to get to this shelling area is to drive onto the beach in your four-wheel drive vehicle. All off-road vehicle (ORV) beach entrances are numbered. The roadside sign, identifying these entrances, has a picture of an ORV, an arrow pointing in the direction of the entrance, and the entrance number. On Ocracoke Island you do not need a permit to drive on the beach and there are no beach fees. Everyone who enjoys driving on the beach must obey the rules and respect the environment so all of us can continue enjoying this privilege.

At ORV entrance #59, drive onto the beach and go to the left. Continue along the beach until you come to the Hatteras Inlet. Looking across the inlet, you will see the southern end of Hatteras Island. This sand spit, jutting out into the inlet, is generally covered with fishermen and their vehicles. If you do not have a four-wheel drive vehicle, park in the lot just south of ORV entrance #59. Walk onto the beach and go to the left. It will be about a mile walk to the shelling spot. You can also park at the ferry lot. Walk down the path through the dunes on the sound side and go to the right. The best shell hunting area at North Point is sound side of the protruding pilings, the remains of an old Coast Guard station destroyed in a 1955 storm.

The rapid turbulent flow of water through Hatteras Inlet carries large amounts of sand and shells. The best time to go shelling here is from about two hours before low tide to just after the tide turns and begins coming in again. Ideally, the water in the inlet should not be rough. You should always check the beach first to see what has been deposited by the receding tide. However, the most productive shelling will be at the water's edge, where small waves lap at the shore. Here you will see whole shells and shell pieces washing around in the water. On a good shelling day you will probably fill two or three gallon-size bags in a couple of hours. Many of the shells will be olives.

Olive shells are cylindrical and elongated with a cone-shaped point on one end. They range in size from one-quarter of an inch to five inches long. Their width is about one-third their length. If olive shells have not been battered by the surf and sand, they are very glossy. When olives are alive, the mollusk's mantle covers the shell completely, cleaning, polishing, and protecting it. This results in the shell's glossy appearance. World-wide there are about 300 species of olives and about 25 species are found in North America (Rehder, 1981.) The Lettered Olive is the species found on Ocracoke. They are more abundant at North Point than anywhere else on the island. Lettered Olives (illustration 12) are usually light gray or beige and have brown zigzag markings. Adult Lettered Olives vary in size from one and three-quarter inches to two and three-quarter inches. The size of olive shells found at North Point range from three-quarters of an inch to two and three-quarter inches long. One day we found thirty-one Lettered Olive shells in excellent condition. We threw back about a hundred olives with minor holes or other flaws.

Olives live and breed in shallow sandy water. They lay their eggs in round capsules, either attaching them to hard objects or releasing them into the water. You often can see the round egg capsules washed up on the beach. Olives feed on small clams and crabs. They

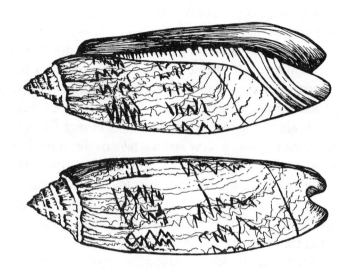

illustration 12   Lettered Olives

wrap part of their body around their victims, dragging them under the sand, where they consume their catch.

Shelling for olives at water's edge requires a keen eye and quick reflexes. Most seashells are flat and slide or tumble around in the surf. Olive shells, being cylindrical, roll like pencils on a slanted surface when waves wash them onto shore. This rolling movement allows you to distinguish olive shells from the others. When you see an olive rolling in the water, quickly grab the shell before it rolls back into the ditch. If you lose sight of it, keep looking in the same area. It will usually roll up again. If you still have not found it after a few more waves, slowly walk down the beach in the direction of the current and continue looking for the shell. If it does not get buried in the ditch, you will probably find it. Besides finding olives in the water, you can also find them in the intertidal zone. They come in with the tide and larger waves, occasionally remaining on the beach.

North Point is also a productive location for finding several other shell species. Medium sized (3-4 inch) Knobbed Whelks, sand dollars, scallops, Common American Augers (illustration 13,) and even Scotch Bonnets are commonly found here. On one outing we were shelling for a few hours when the tide began coming in. Within about ten minutes a stiff onshore wind began pushing sea grass onto shore. This was accompanied by the tinkling sound created by shells hitting against shells. An unusually productive shelling experience followed as we found five Scotch Bonnets and a small Queen Helmet within the next half hour.

Scotch Bonnets at "Bonnet Beach"

Bonnet Beach is located ocean-side, approximately mid-island. To our knowledge this area does not have a

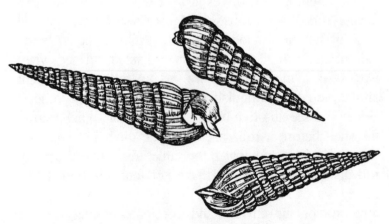

illustration 13 Common American Augers

name, so we call it "Bonnet Beach." It is the location of our most prosperous bonnet shelling. The method used for shelling on Bonnet Beach is to stroll the beach at low tide, searching through everything washed up during the previous high tide. You can even find bonnet shells at the high water lines of previous high tides.

There are three ways to get to Bonnet Beach. If you have an off-road vehicle, drive onto the beach at entrance #67 and go to the left. Note, this beach entrance is sometimes closed because of beach erosion or flooding. Park at the signs instructing you not to drive any farther. Walk about a half-mile northeast, up the beach, and you will be there. Another option is to park at the Pony Pasture Beach parking lot. Walk onto the beach and go to the right for about a mile and a half. You will then be at Bonnet Beach. Your other choice is to park at Parker's Creek on Route 12 and take the sand path over the dunes, through the mosquito and green fly infested brush. If you're sensitive to bug bites, you may not want to opt for this route. The path enters the beach about a mile south of the Pony Pasture. Once on the beach, turn right and walk until you are about half way to the signs informing ORV operators they cannot drive any farther. This is Bonnet Beach. Whichever route you take, you will come to an area of beach having many pieces of shells in the intertidal zone. In this area you will also notice the beach is wider and very gently sloped. This topography allows whole bonnet shells to wash unbroken onto the beach.

The Scotch Bonnet is the state shell of North Carolina. It is harder to find than the whelk, olive, cockle, or scallop shell. This mollusk lives on the sand in shallow water and lays its eggs in a tall, round, tower-like column. The bonnet feeds on sea urchins and sand dollars. It extracts the meat of these animals by boring holes in their hard covering.

When you see a Scotch Bonnet (illustration 14) its beauty will intrigue you. It is a delicate shell in both appearance and structure. Their natural color is pale yellow/white with rows of darker tan square spots, but you will also find them white, light gray, dark gray, black, dark brown, and beige. The shell is somewhat oval, narrower at one end and pointed at the other. When you find a whole bonnet, it is most often positioned with its opening on the sand and its round profile toward the sky. Usually, if it is sitting on the beach upside down or on end, it is not whole. You will see the pointed end is broken off or it has a hole in its delicate rounded side. However, its beauty will call you

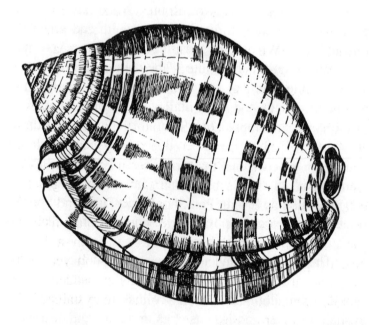

illustration 14   Scotch Bonnet

over for a closer inspection, and if you are lucky, it just might be a "keeper." A week long stay on Ocracoke might net a novice sheller one Scotch Bonnet shell in good condition. With bonnet shelling knowledge and experience, it is possible to find many more. On a one week trip, we will find about twenty Scotch Bonnets in good condition. Storms bring many more Scotch Bonnetts onto shore. After hurricane Fran in 1996, we found 483 bonnet shells in only one week. A shelling frenzy for sure!

A beach collectible to look for at low tide is the sea star. While shelling at Bonnet Beach one October, we found a sea star measuring nine inches across. It was dead, so we carefully carried it back with us. We also observed a five-inch sea star, royal purple with a pale yellow outline around its perimeter. It was beautiful and quite alive. The tentacles on its underside were moving around as if it were trying to tickle our hands when we picked it up. We carefully put it back into the sea.

When shelling, you can also observe other interesting objects on the beach and enjoy many different experiences. One thing to look for is pieces of rock resembling broken cement. Some of the pieces will have shells embedded in them. These rock pieces break off from a major rock bed that underlies much of the North Carolina coast. This bed occurs in all the big shoals offshore such as Frying Pan Shoals and Diamond Shoals. It provides important hardbottom habitat for fish and shellfish. One sample we found was from a former beach deposit estimated to be 1 to 2 million years old. We were also informed that the shells embedded in our sample were highly dissolved and recrystallized by ground water processes.

Something else to observe is sand composed of heavy minerals. Most commonly seen as black sand, it is particularly evident after storms, high up in the intertidal zone. Several years ago after two tropical storms had passed by offshore, we found a very large deposit of this sand near the Pony Pen beach. It was very beautiful as it contained a lot of red sand, too. Recently, we had our sample analyzed and were informed these sands are common sediments, extremely stable, and stay around for millions of years. They consist of illmenite and magnetite (black,) garnet (red,) zircon topaz and tourmaline (light greens, blues, yellows,) among others.

An exciting experience on Ocracoke is observing dolphin swimming very close to shore. They are easier to see on days when the sun is high in the sky and the surf is calm. One day we were fortunate to be able to swim with these graceful animals. As we were diving under a wave, several dolphin began riding the wave alongside us. We encourage you to take breaks from intense shelling to observe your surroundings, so you too can enjoy the varied aspects of nature.

"Shell Banks" at South Point

Another productive shelling area on Ocracoke is at the south end of the island, called South Point. The best way to get to this shelling spot is to enter the beach at ORV entrance #72. This entrance is located north of the Sheriff's office, on the same side of the street. The drive out on the sand road is three miles. Although this road is sandy, it is sometimes hard packed and cars do negotiate it. However, the road is more often very soft sand, dotted with large water-filled ditches. Drivers of vehicles not having four-wheel drive should be especially cautious and attentive to the condition of the road. Towing on the island is limited!

The scenery on the ride out to the beach is breathtaking. At the beginning of the journey there will be trees and bushes, with cattails indicating the fresh water line. For the balance of the ride you will see acres and acres of grasses. Depending on the season, the colors of these grasses will vary to include all shades of greens, reds, and browns. Intermixed with the grasses are flowering plants of white and yellow. You will also observe pelicans, egrets, herons, terns, gulls, and a variety of other birds.

After going out the road for almost three miles, the road curves to the left. If you have driven out in a vehicle without four-wheel drive, park before you come to soft sand. Once on the beach go to the right and walk or drive along the water's edge. From here to "The Point" you will have the opportunity to do a lot of shelling.

Another route to South Point is to park at the airport, ORV entrance #70. Walk the short distance out the sand road, over the dune, and turn right at the ocean. You will then have to walk about three miles to South Point.

Where the three-mile sand road comes onto the beach, you will usually see thousands of pieces of shells in groups or mounds. They are found at the water's edge as the tide goes out. We refer to these groups of shells as "shell banks." As waves wash over the piles of shells, keep looking for whole shells and Keyhole Urchins to appear. Take time to search through these mounds and you will be surprised how many shells you can find. At South Point you can find most of the varieties of shells common to Ocracoke.   Your best shelling will be in the intertidal and subtidal zones.   The most exciting experience we have had at this shelling area was when we found 472 bleached white Keyhole Urchins in one week.   On many days we had to awake before sunrise to take advantage of the best tide.   We went shelling two hours before low tide, and as the tide was going out, it seemed like each wave uncovered another Keyhole Urchin.   They ranged in size from three-quarters of an inch to an inch and a quarter in diameter.

Urchins are very fragile.   One day while we were fishing with some friends, one of them picked up a small Keyhole Urchin uncovered by a wave lapping at his feet. He gave it to his sister and, without thinking, she put the fragile find into her jeans pocket.   It did not survive.   On another occasion, we put a two-inch diameter Keyhole Urchin in an empty sneaker to keep it safe until we got back to our cottage.   Several hours later, forgetting about the urchin, we slapped the sneakers together to remove the sand from the soles of the shoes.   We could not imagine what the unusual noise was.   Suddenly, we realized the urchin was no longer in one piece.

After you have searched for shells and Keyhole Urchins at the three-mile road beach area, continue south and you will come to the end of the island.   This sand spit is also a popular gathering spot for fishermen.   With their four-wheel drive vehicles lined up at water's edge, they will have several fishing lines out.   The fishermen usually do not interfere with your shelling.   However, on occasion, they park and fish right over what appears to be a great shelling spot.   Since they were there first, cautiously shell around them.   Be very careful when walking on the ocean side of a fishing pole.   You do not want to be the catch of the day. It would not make you or the fishermen very happy.

At the end of the sand spit, stroll the beach and look for areas where there are shell banks. You should also look for signs of whelk and Queen Helmet shells buried in the sand or left in the ditches at low tide. Whelk and helmet shells can also be found in the shallow water here. Walk in the water and look for shells or feel for them with your feet. Most of the time only a small portion of a whole shell will be exposed. If you are lucky, you may even experience the thrill of a large whelk shell washing up on the beach right in front of you.

Be exceptionally cautious when shelling in the water at South Point. With every tide change, a huge volume of water is funneled between Ocracoke and neighboring Portsmith Island. The resulting currents are extremely treacherous.

Although a relatively small island, Ocracoke offers shellers the opportunity to find many varieties of shells, using several shell hunting techniques, under varied beach conditions. Whether you spend a day, a weekend, or a week or two, if you love nature, you will love Ocracoke Island.

6

Chincoteague and Assateague Islands, Virginia

Chincoteague and Assateague Islands are located just off the coast of the Delmarva Peninsula. The Delmarva Peninsula has the Delaware Bay to the northeast, the Atlantic Ocean to the east, and the Chesapeake Bay to the west. The peninsula is within the boundaries of Delaware, Maryland, and Virginia, resulting in the name "Delmarva." To get to Chincoteague National Wildlife Refuge and the Tom's Cove section of Assateague Island, Virginia, travel on Route 13, and in Oak Hall, take Route 175 east to Chincoteague. It is about a fifteen-minute ride from Route 13. You will pass NASA's Wallop Island Flight Center and travel over beautiful salt marsh. When you get to the traffic light, turn left, and follow the signs to Assateague Island.

Chincoteague, a quaint fishing village, is the gateway to the Chincoteague National Wildlife Refuge and the Tom's Cove section of Assateague Island National Seashore. The island is well known for its oyster beds and clam shoals. Chincoteague's famous Salt Oysters, sold since 1830, are cultivated on leased public property. The watermen seed and harvest their beds similar to farmers planting and harvesting their fields.

The Chincoteague National Wildlife Refuge, located on Assateague Island, is managed by the Fish and Wildlife Service, U. S. Department of the Interior. Established in 1943 as a wintering area for migratory waterfowl, the refuge is essential to the survival of birds whose migrational instincts annually take them north and south on their remarkable journeys. If you like bird watching and shelling, this refuge is the place to visit. Over 250 species of birds can be identified here, and as fall temperatures turn colder, thousands upon thousands of Canada Geese, Snow Geese, and swans usher in winter.

This wildlife refuge is also home to the legendary Chincoteague wild ponies. According to legend, centuries ago horses swam ashore from wrecked Spanish galleons and the ponies are their descendants. However, it is more realistic to believe the ponies are descendants of horses left behind by early settlers. In the 17th century settlers raised their domesticated stock on the island. They grazed their horses here to avoid fencing requirements and the taxes they would have to pay if they grazed them on the mainland. Visit the Chincoteague Refuge Visitor Center and pick up brochures explaining all the refuge wildlife. The visitor center also provides schedules for guided walks and auditorium programs. There are many other activities to enjoy on Chincoteague including boating, swimming, crabbing, fishing, and biking or hiking the nature trails.

Managed by the National Park Service, Assateague Island has thirty-seven miles of natural, unspoiled beaches. Twenty-two miles of beach are in Maryland and fifteen are in Virginia. The Virginia section protects Chincoteague from the crashing surf of the Atlantic Ocean. Assateague is constantly being reshaped by waves, steady winds, and storms. Sand, washed up from the gently sloping ocean floor by persistent wave action, helps to create the beach and dunes. Behind the dunes you will find forests, bays, and marshes.

While visiting Assateague Island, stop at Tom's Cove Visitor Center to see beach life exhibits and to pick up maps, brochures, and other literature. Also ask about the seashore and wildlife programs. They include guided walks exploring bird habitats, the salt marshes, the bay, dunes, and beaches. You can also take part in nature presentations about birds, marshes, barrier islands, and beachcombing. Seashore demonstrations are available and include surf rescue and surf fishing.

Shelling on Assateague Island National Seashore

Tom's Cove section of Assateague Island, Virginia, offers an exciting shelling experience. The best shelling is on the southern end of Tom's Cove Hook (map 3.) Park at the southernmost beach parking area. Once on the beach, turn right and walk one and a half miles. You will then be at the whelk shelling area. Here, the island begins to hook around toward Chincoteague Inlet.

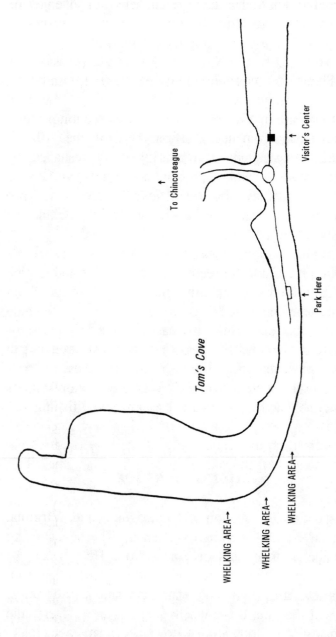

map 3 Tom's Cove Hook, Assateague Island, Virginia

WHELKING AREA→

WHELKING AREA→

WHELKING AREA→

Tom's Cove

To Chincoteague

Park Here

Visitor's Center

Atlantic Ocean

The contour of the beach, the currents, and the gentle slope of the ocean floor are several reasons why whelk shells are abundant here.

Shells Commonly Found on Assateague Island:

Knobbed Whelk	Atlantic Bay Scallop
Channeled Whelk	Blue Mussel
Lightning Whelk	Shark Eye
Northern Quahog	Common American Auger
Coquina Shell	Soft-shell Clam
Ponderous Ark	Atlantic Jackknife Clam
Atlantic Surf Clam	
Atlantic Ribbed Mussel	
Common Atlantic Slipper Shell	
Common Northern Moon Shell	
Eastern Oyster (Virginia's State Shell)	

The whelk shell most commonly found on Assateague Island is the Knobbed Whelk. Other whelk shells found here are the Lightning Whelk and Channeled Whelk. The adult Knobbed Whelk (illustration 15) is generally four to nine inches long, measured from point to point. The width of the large end of the shell is about half the size of its length. This whelk has a large opening. When held with the knobbed end pointing up, the opening of the shell will generally be on the right. However, some Knobbed Whelks do have the opening on the left. The prominent ridges running from point to point are formed as the shell grows. The Knobbed Whelk has a low cone shaped spire and the whirl of the spire has rounded knobs. These knobs give this whelk its name. Knobbed Whelk shells found on the beach are usually a light beige, pale grayish-white, or

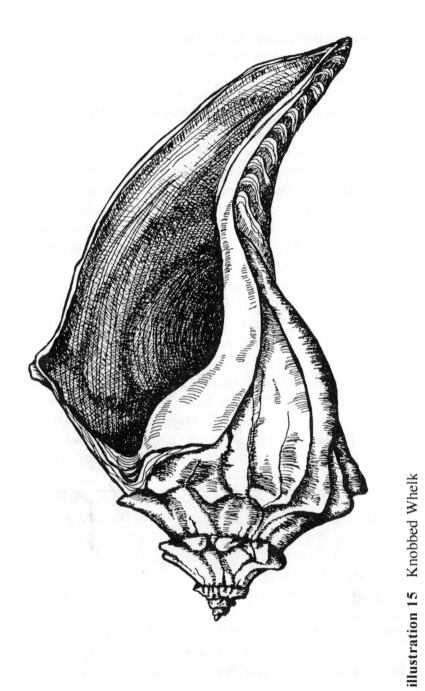

illustration 15 Knobbed Whelk

dark gray. Sometimes, inside the shell's opening, the color of the shell will be a deep orange.

The Lightning Whelk (illustration 16) is very similar to the Knobbed Whelk, but the knobs are very low. The opening of the Lightning Whelk is on the left. The shell is whitish and has dark brown or rust color axial streaks, or stripes, from point to point. The Channeled Whelk (illustration 17) is also similar in shape and size to the Knobbed Whelk. Instead of knobs on the whirl of the spire, it has what looks like a band of small beads. If the shell is worn, these beads may not be noticeable. The Channeled Whelk's opening is on the right.

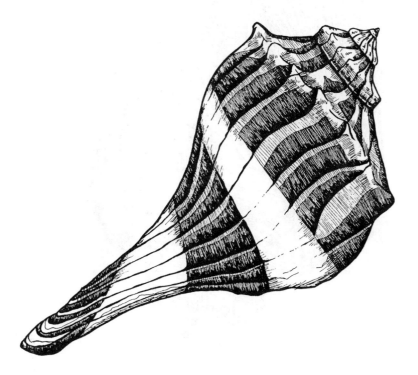

illustration 16 Lightning Whelk

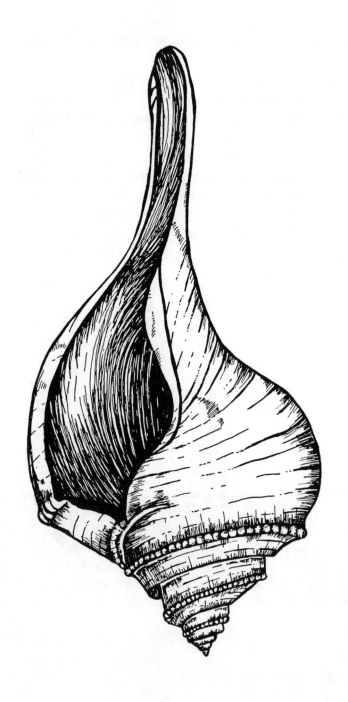

illustration 17   Channeled Whelk

Whelk shells found on the beach are usually empty. Occasionally, when found in the water or wet sand they will contain the live animal. You will then have the opportunity to see the mollusk's large fleshy orange body extended from its shell. Once disturbed, the animal will retreat into the shell for protection. When you are finished observing the whelk, carefully place it back into the water so it can continue to live, grow, and produce more beautiful whelk.

"Whelking"

We call looking for whelk shells "whelking." In a two-hour whelking expedition, the potential exists for finding fifty to sixty whole whelk shells. However, the National Park Service limits the amount of shells you can carry off the beach on any one visit to what will fit in a one-gallon container. The Fish and Wildlife Service allows shellers to take a half bushel per person. Also, shells found on the island may not be sold or used for any commercial purpose.

There are many methods used to find whelk shells. The easiest method is to stroll the beach and look for shells washing up with the tide or left behind by the previous tide. The best time to go whelking is two hours before low tide, to low tide. Whelk shells can also be found in the shallow water of the subtidal zone. The shells roll around in the water, collect sand in their openings, and become buried in the sand. Often, the rounded knobbed area of a whelk can be seen crowning out of the sand. Sometimes the shell will be barely noticeable. When you find a "crowning" whelk, dig into the sand around it and pull out the shell. Then rinse the shell out. You will think you have given it a good rinsing, but sand will fall out for what will seem like forever.

In the intertidal zone you will usually see pools of water. Search in these pools for whelk shells. In the subtidal zone, walk out into ankle to knee-deep water. The whelk shells are large enough to be seen under the water, where they collect in ditches created by the waves and currents. Sandbars should also be checked for shells left behind by the receding tide.

Using your off-road vehicle (ORV) to go whelking provides easy access to the best shelling area. There is a yearly ORV beach fee for Assateague Island. To obtain an ORV permit by mail, write to the Assateague Island National Seashore, National Park Service in Berlin, Maryland, and request an application. You may also obtain a permit in person at the Seashore Visitor Center or the Refuge Headquarters on Assateague Island. Important! The whelking area is also the nesting habitat for the endangered piping plover. To aid in the recovery of this species, the area is subject to closure during the nesting season, March 15 to August 31. When planning your trip, it is best to call ahead to see if the area is closed, or schedule your shelling trip during the months of September through February.

Other shells you will probably find while whelking include scallop, snail, oyster, and several varieties of clam. Oyster shells found here are generally much bigger than oyster shells found on other East Coast beaches. Sometimes they can be found ten to twelve inches in length.

Other Beach Collectibles on Assateague Island

As you explore the beach, you will find other beach collectibles. Obvious, but often overlooked, is the sand. Sand on beaches from northern Florida, north through Massachusetts, is similar in color and texture. It is usually light tan or whitish with granules about the size of table sugar. The sand originated thousands of years ago when moving glaciers, about a mile thick, crushed the rocks in their path. The movement of a tremendous volume of water crushed rocks against rocks, pulverizing them into fine particles. The smallest particles were carried down rivers and streams. Eventually these particles were carried into the ocean, creating beaches. Assateague Island sand is composed of rock fragments from the Appalachian Mountains and areas even farther inland, possibly from the center of the continent.

Sand on the beach appears slightly different closer to the dunes than at water's edge. Waves and wind carry sand and, as the sand moves, the individual granules become sorted according to weight and size. The heavier and bigger particles often get deposited first and do not travel as far as smaller or lighter particles. The wind carries the smallest particles even farther up onto the beach. This results in finer sand near the dunes than in the often wet intertidal zone. Sand at the dunes is sometimes a darker gray when it is mixed with particles of decayed vegetation and other debris bound together with organic matter and silt.

Whelk shell egg cases are another common collectible found on the beach at Assateague Island. They resemble spinal columns. These strings of disks, one to two feet in length, are usually found parchment-like, very dry and yellowish. However, if found freshly washed onto the beach, they are soft and whitish. Every disk of these columns is an egg case containing up to 100 young whelk shells. If the column of egg cases washed up before the mollusks were mature enough to break out, you will hear the little shells rattling around inside when you shake the column. Cut an egg case open and you will find many whelk shells, each about the size of a dull pencil point. If you have the patience to cut open several disks, you can fill a small display jar, creating a very interesting conversation piece.

Also abundant on Assateague Island is the horseshoe crab. Although called a crab, it is not a crab but a marine arthropod. Its closest relative was a spider, extinct for millions of years. This animal is a dark brown, horseshoe shaped, convex creature, with a spike tail. Often considered poisonous or harmful, the crab will not sting if you touch it. Actually, the horseshoe crab uses its tail to right itself when it becomes flipped over. On the East Coast, the horseshoe crab's habitat extends from Florida to Maine. Horseshoe crabs live in shallow coastal waters. They molt their skeletons to grow, sometimes up to twenty inches long. This neatly shed skeleton is a regular find on Assateague Island.

When you visit Chincoteague and Assateague Islands, besides finding shells, you have many opportunities to learn about seashore life. Through nature presentations and direct observation, you will develop a good understanding of the ever-changing beach environment.

7

New Jersey

Coastal New Jersey is the summer vacation destination of many New York, Pennsylvania, and northern New Jersey residents. The Jersey Shore is one of the most popular resort areas in the United States. Visitors are attracted here by the 127 miles of white sandy beaches, barrier islands, beautiful bays, the Intracoastal Waterway, and Atlantic Ocean. New Jersey offers visitors water activities including clamming, crabbing, sport and surf fishing, boating, water skiing, snorkeling, surfing, deep-sea diving, and shelling.

The Delaware River flows along the west side of the state, separating New Jersey from Pennsylvania. The Atlantic Ocean borders the central and southern sections of eastern New Jersey. Along the state's coastline there are several parks with sandy beaches. Gateway National Recreation Area, Sandy Hook, is located on the northern portion of the coast, just across the bay from New York City. Island Beach State Park and Barnegat Lighthouse State Park are situated midway on the coast, and Cape May Point State Park is at the southern tip of the state.

New Jersey's heritage developed out of its close relationship with the ocean.   The coastal area from Sandy Hook to Cape May and north along the Delaware River to Deepwater, was designated the New Jersey Coastal Heritage Trail in 1988.   The heritage trail was established "to provide for public appreciation, education, understanding, and enjoyment" of cultural and natural sites associated with this coastal area.   The trail is divided into five regions.   Within the regions the themes that define the aspects of life here include historic settlements, vacation destinations, maritime history, wildlife migration, and coastal habitats.

Shelling at the Jersey Shore

New Jersey's beaches offer an interesting variety of shelling experiences.   Shells can be found on all beaches.   You can also find a variety of beach collectibles.   Locations discussed in this chapter include Gateway National Recreation Area at Sandy Hook, Belmar, Manasquan, Barnegat Lighthouse State Park, Great Egg Harbor Inlet, Hereford Inlet, and Cape May.

Shells Commonly Found in New Jersey:

Blue Mussel	Atlantic Jackknife Clam
Shark Eye	Common Periwinkle
Ribbed Mussel	Atlantic Surf Clam
Northern Quahog	Common Jingle Shell
Eastern Oyster	Atlantic Bay Scallop
False Angel Wing	Minor Jackknife Clam
Channeled Whelk	Smooth Astarte
Soft-shell Clam	
Eastern Mud Whelk	

Common Atlantic Slipper Shell
Common Northern Moon Shell
Knobbed Whelk (New Jersey's State Shell)

An unusual find on New Jersey's beaches is the Ponderous Ark. The shell species' range is from Virginia to Florida and Texas, where the water is warmer. The shells found in New Jersey could be fossil shells washed out from fossil beds, as the Ponderous Ark inhabited this area when the water here was warmer.

Moon Shells and Jingle Shells at Sandy Hook

Gateway National Recreation Area, Sandy Hook, is a peninsula extending six and a half miles into the Atlantic Ocean near the entrance to New York Harbor. New York City's magnificent skyline can be seen from the park's northernmost beach. Sandy Hook's location has made it an important navigational landmark since the 1600's. During the time of the American Revolution and until 1974, this area was a key defense site protecting New York City from possible enemy attack.

Sandy Hook is the New Jersey section of Gateway National Recreation Area. It is administered by the National Park Service, U.S. Department of the Interior. In 1972, Congress created Gateway National Recreation Area, providing parkland around New York Harbor. The harbor has been the "Gateway" for millions of immigrants entering the United States. Sandy Hook was designated a National Historic Landmark in 1982. The peninsula's natural landscape is protected by sand dunes. The dunes help vegetation to grow by blocking the area behind the dune line from ocean winds and storms.

Sandy Hook is located north of Highlands. From the Garden State Parkway, take exit 117 to Route 36 east and travel for about fourteen miles. When you arrive at Highlands, follow the signs to Sandy Hook. When you enter the park, continue north to the Visitors' Center. Stop and ask for directions to the parking area near the northernmost battery bunkers. From this parking area walk north to the end of the bunkers and follow the sand path to the beach.

On the beach you can find the shells of the Common Atlantic Slipper Shell, Knobbed Whelk, Channeled Whelk, Blue Mussel, and several species of clams. The Common Northern Moon Shell (illustration 18,) also called Moon Snail, can be found in abundance. As you walk toward the bay, there are many empty Moon

illustration 18   Common Northern Moon Shell

Snail shells washed up on the beach. On calm days at low tide, it is also possible to observe live Moon Snails extended from their shell in the shallow water. When extended from their shells, these mollusks look like jellyfish with a snail shell riding on top. The animal is much larger than its shell because it has inflated with water (illustration 19.) To retract into the shell, the mollusks expel the water.

The aperture, or opening of the univalve, where the mollusk extends its head and foot, is semicircular. The aperture is closed by the operculum, or "trap door," when the snail retreats into the shell. The operculum of the Moon Snail is thin, semicircular, brown, with a dull luster. When beach strolling, you will find many opercula. After cleaning Moon Snail shells, you can stuff the opening of the shells with paper and glue the trap doors back in place for display purposes.

Another beach collectible from the Moon Snail is a sand collar. The snail mixes its eggs with sand and a gelatin material, forming a very fragile cone-shaped collar. The collar has a wide opening at the bottom and a smaller opening at the top. These collars can be found in calm bay waters and washed up on the beach. Sand collars are flexible when wet and hard when dry. They break very easily and must be handled gently. To protect them for display, brush the underside with water-base transparent glue or spray them with lacquer.

A shell often misidentified as a Common Northern Moon Shell is the Shark Eye (illustration 20.) There are several visible differences between the species. The Moon Shell is larger, almost round, with a height of one and one-half inches to five inches, compared to the Shark Eye's domed shaped seven-eighths inch to three inch size. Moon Shells found at Sandy Hook are gray-

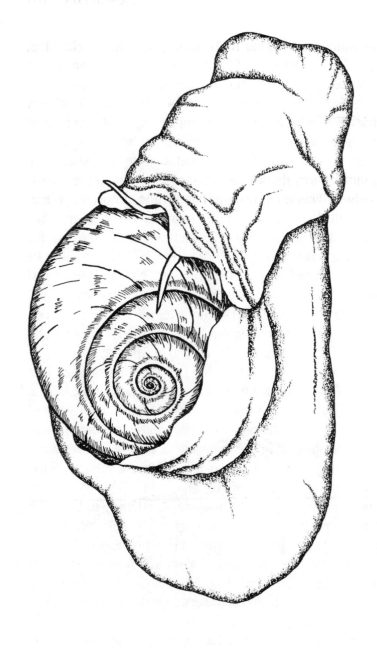

illustration 19 Common Northern Moon Shell (live)

ish-white with whorls of brown, dark blue, light blue, and light yellow. The Shark Eyes are bluish to brownish-gray with chestnut brown. They are much darker than Moon Shells. The early whorls are very dark. Encircled by consecutive paler whorls, the darkest area appears to be an eye. The most distinguishing difference between the two shells is the umbilicus, an opening at the base of the pillar around which the whorls revolve. This area of the Shark Eye is almost complete- ly covered with a whitish to chestnut brown pad. The umbilicus of the Moon Snail is deep and almost completely open.

Common Jingle Shells, also called "Mermaids' Toenails," are another beautiful find at Sandy Hook. Bend down, look closely, and you will see them scat- tered along the beach at the high tide line. These shells

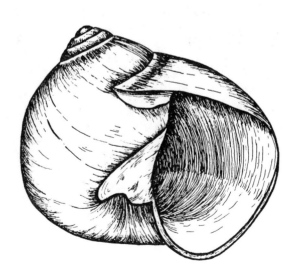

illustration 20 Shark Eye

are irregularly circular, thin, and translucent. They have a pearly appearance and are yellow, orange, black, or silver. Jingle shells have fine growth lines and appear wrinkled. They range in size from one-half inch to two and one-quarter inches in diameter. Most of the jingle shells found here are about three-quarters of an inch to one inch in diameter. Jingle shells are bivalves. The left valve is convex and thicker than the right valve.

The flat, fragile right valve has a hole near its hinge for the byssus. When the mollusk is alive, the right shell is firmly attached to rocks, other shells, or pilings, by the calcified byssus. The right shell usually does not break free. The left half is the shell generally found washed ashore. It is possible, although rare, to find the left and right valves attached. Common Jingle Shells are very attractive when displayed in clear glass jars or put out for show in a shell shaped dish.

Strolling the beach can result in many other finds at Sandy Hook. You will find shells to include Atlantic Jackknife Clams, Atlantic Surf Clams, Northern Quahogs, Blue Mussels, and Common Periwinkles. The Atlantic Jackknife Clam (illustration 21) is an unusual clam because of its shape. It is oblong, slightly curved, with both ends squared off. The exterior of the shell is white and the periostracum is olive green. It has fine vertical growth lines, with the growth lines on one end being very prominent. The Atlantic Jackknife Clam lives in the intertidal zone where it burrows vertically into the sand. The Minor Jackknife Clam, a similar smaller species, is also found here.

Finding Sharks' Teeth in Belmar

Belmar is located south of Asbury Park between Avon and Spring Lake. From the Garden State Parkway take exit 98 and travel east on Route 138 to Highway 35 north. Exit Highway 35 north onto 10th Avenue. Continue east for approximately one mile to Ocean Avenue. Turn left and drive to the Shark River Inlet. Park near the Belmar fishing pier. If you visit here between Memorial Day and Labor Day, you must purchase a "beach badge" to access the beach. Enter the beach to the right of the fishing pier. The best area for finding sharks' teeth is from the pier to the inlet. The beach in

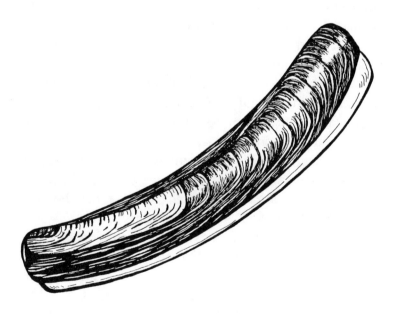

illustration 21 Atlantic Jackknife Clam

the intertidal zone usually has an area consisting of larger grains of sand at the high tide line. This is the best place to look for the fossilized sharks' teeth. They range in size from less than one-half inch to three-quarters of an inch. The teeth are small, so you will need to be patient and focused when looking for them. Most of the teeth will be found on top of the sand.

The beach here is also a good shelling location even in the summer because it is left in a natural condition. Since it is not groomed every day, shells are left on the beach for you to collect.

Observing Sea Stars at the Manasquan Inlet

From Belmar take Highway 35 south to Highway 71 south and travel approximately five miles. In Manasquan, turn left onto East Main Street and continue east to First Avenue. Turn right onto First Avenue and proceed to the inlet.

Manasquan Inlet is the northern end of the Intra-coastal Waterway and one of the busiest inlets on the East Coast. The first beach north of the inlet is a favorite surfing spot, well known by serious East Coast surfers. During the winter months, several species of northern shore birds take up residence in the inlet, as does the occasional seal. In spring, the Forbes' Common Sea Star makes its appearance.

Forbes' Common Sea Stars (illustration 22) are usually seen on rocks or in tide pools at low tide. You may have called them "starfish." However, they are not fish and biologists suggest we call them sea stars. The most obvious characteristic of sea stars is their radial symmetry. A characteristic seen in all members of the Phylum Echinodermata, including sea urchins and sand

dollars.   Sea stars are star shaped with five arms, also
called rays.   They are about three inches to five inches
across and are shades of orange to brown.   The bright
orange spot on top of the animal is a perforated disk
called a sieve plate.   A feature unique to Echinoderms is
a water vascular system.   This internal hydraulic system
operates the many tube feet the animal uses for
locomotion and feeding.   Inside the sea star's body is a
complex network of canals filled with seawater.   The
water needed to operate the vascular system is drawn
and expelled through the sieve plate.

   To observe Forbes' Common Sea Stars alive in
their environment, visit the Manasquan Inlet at low tide
and look over the railing.   You will see them suctioned

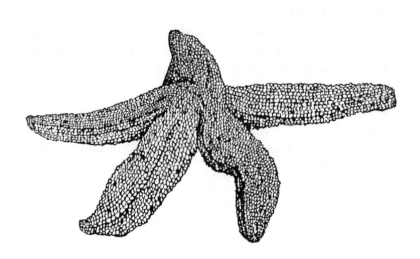

illustration 22 Forbes' Common Sea Star

to rocks as they wait for the next high tide. The size of sea stars is related to the amount of food they eat and not their age. They are smaller in spring and larger in late summer. In winter sea stars shrink in size and inhabit deeper waters.

The Forbes' Common Sea Star feeds on oysters, quahogs, mussels, scallops, and snails. They grab onto their prey using their strong tentacles and tube feet. Scientists have conducted studies that determine a Forbes' Common Sea Star three inches in radius can exert a twelve-pound pull. A small two inch quahog can only exert a ten-pound pull to keep its valves closed tight. The sea star wins the tug-of-war. It needs only a 1/250 inch opening between the mollusk's two valves to begin its meal. Amazingly, the sea star turns its stomach inside out through its mouth. It then slides the stomach through the tiny opening and begins to secrete digestive juices. The clam dies. The valves then open wide and the sea star enjoys a feast.

Do not disturb live sea stars. If you would like to have one for your collection, you can find them washed up on the sandy beach after they have died naturally.

Barnegat Lighthouse State Park

Barnegat Lighthouse State Park is located at the northern tip of Long Beach Island. Exit the Garden State Parkway at exit 63 and take Route 72 east to Long Beach Boulevard north. Continue to the northern end of the island. At the inlet, you will see an entrance sign for the park. You will also see "Old Barney," one of the more popular lighthouses on the Atlantic Coast. This attractive 165 foot tall red and white structure was refurbished to its original splendor in 1988.

Either before or after visiting the lighthouse, walk along the jetty to the ocean. As you walk, look for shells at the high tide line and in the water near the jetty. You will probably find many very large moon snail opercula. Also look closely to find the small Eastern Mud Whelk. On one occasion, we passed a woman who had collected almost a gallon size bag of these pretty shells. As you approach the ocean beach, you may find many pieces of large colorful moon shells. Keep searching and you might find beautiful whole ones.

Several species of clam shells, the most common find on New Jersey beaches, are easy to find here. Atlantic Surf Clams (illustration 23) are fun to pick up and admire because of their size. Often they grow to seven inches across. Children love to play with them. They also enjoy taking them home to color or paint.

The exterior of surf clam shells are yellowish-white or grayish. When the mollusks are alive, their shells are covered with a grayish-yellow periostracum. The shells become very white after being bleached by the sun. The inside is smooth and the outside has concentric growth lines. The Atlantic Surf Clam lives just below the low tide line, to water 140 feet deep. Another species similar to the Atlantic Surf Clam is the Northern Quahog (illustration 24.) Quahogs are found in sheltered bays and coves. These clams burrow in mud and sand, in a mix of fresh and salt water at the low tide line. Quahogs are well known for the purple coloring on the inside of their shells.

Because surf clams and quahogs are generalized as "clams," confusion often exists when people talk about them. The easiest way to determine which shell you have found is to look at the hinge area. Quahogs are curved at the hinge and surf clams are more gently

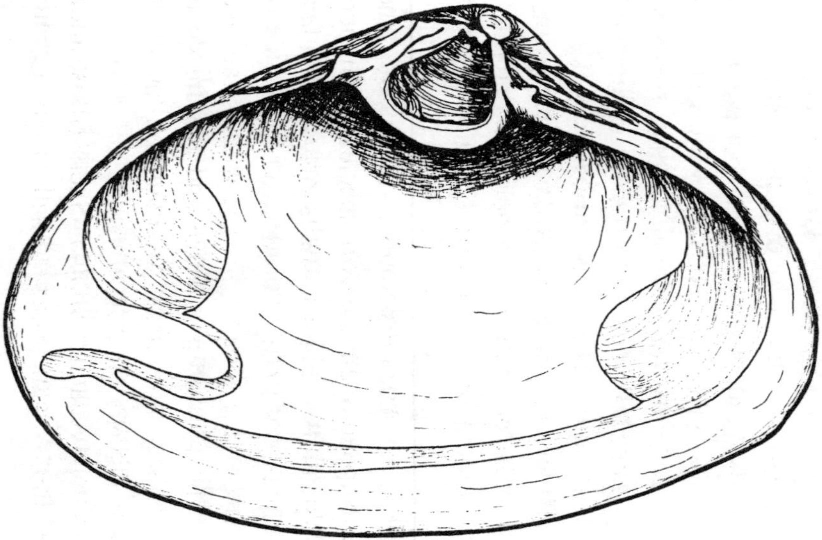

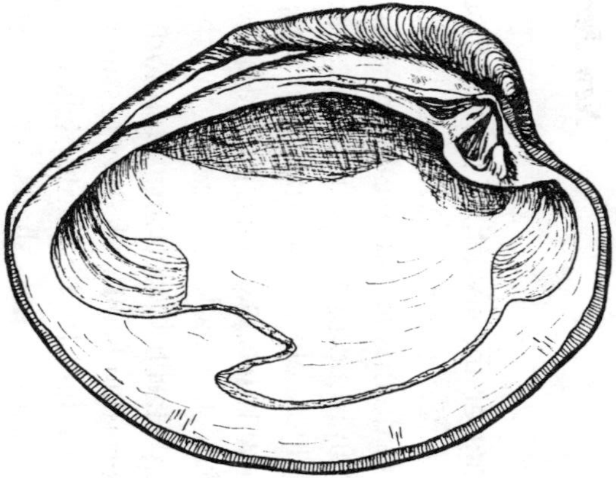

illustration 24 Northern Quahog

illustration 23 Atlantic Surf Clam

rounded. Looking at the inside of the shell where the hinge is located, surf clams have a triangular indentation resembling a miniature surf clam and quahogs do not (compare illustrations 23 and 24.)

Great Egg Harbor Inlet and Hereford Inlet

Great Egg Harbor Inlet and Hereford Inlet are located on barrier islands off the southeastern shore of the Jersey Cape. They are excellent shelling locations. The exchange of water from the Atlantic Ocean to and from the sounds carries a large number of shells and deposits them on the sandy beaches. At both locations you will be able to collect most of the species of shells found in New Jersey.

The Great Egg Harbor Inlet is located at the northern end of Ocean City. To get there, travel the Garden State Parkway to Route 52 into Ocean City (9th Street.) Then go north on Wesley Avenue, which turns into Gardens Parkway. The beach parking lot is just south of the toll bridge on Gardens Parkway. After walking onto the beach, follow it around to the right. You will find shells at the water's edge and at the high tide line.

The Common Atlantic Slipper Shell and the Eastern White Slipper Shell are two species of slippers found at this location. Slipper shells are of the few gastropods that are not spiraled in shape.

The Eastern White Slipper Shell is white, flat, and oval shaped. The outside is smooth and the inside is glossy white. They are often misidentified as worn pieces of broken shell by the casual sheller.

The Common Atlantic Slipper Shell (illustration 25,) also called the Atlantic Slipper Shell, found on this

illustration 25 Common Atlantic Slipper Shells

beach, is larger than others we have found in New Jersey. Most were resting on the beach upside down. Our attention was drawn to the beautiful burgundy color inside the shells. The outsides of the shells were whitish with irregular brownish blotches or radiating lines. These shells are sometimes called Boat Shells because of their appearance. When upside down, they can float on water and look like little boats.

Hereford Inlet is located at the south end of Stone Harbor. Take Garden State Parkway exit 10B, travel on Route 657 east (96th Street) and make a right turn onto Second Avenue. This will take you to the "Stone Harbor Beaches" parking lot. Access the beach by walking down the sand road toward the inlet. Once on the beach you will see a large expanse of sand covered with shells. Shark Eyes, Knobbed Whelks, Channeled Whelks, and Atlantic Jackknife Clams are some of the many species of shells easily found here.

Cape May Diamonds

Cape May is located at the southernmost tip of a thirty-mile long peninsula. The peninsula juts out into the Atlantic Ocean and Delaware Bay. The area has a variety of environments including barrier islands, beaches, bays, fresh water and tidal wetlands, tidal creeks, and streams. When you arrive in Cape May, you may suddenly forget what century you are living in. The city has over 600 authentically restored and preserved Victorian structures. The entire city has been designated a National Historic Landmark. Cape May is also known as the Eastern Flyway, one of the "Dozen Birding Hotspots" in the United States. In the spring and fall seasons, Cape May skies are heavily traveled by migratory birds, with over 400 species recorded by the Audubon Society's Cape May Bird Observatory.

During World War I, a shortage of steel prompted the building of twelve experimental concrete ships. An interesting Cape May attraction is the Atlantus, a concrete ship designated a New Jersey historic site. The ship's construction consisted of concrete five inches thick, reinforced by steel rods. This 250-foot vessel weighed 3,000 tons. The Atlantus was put into service as a coal steamer, but was decommissioned because of its weight and slow speed. A few years after it was decommissioned, the ship was towed to Cape May to be used as a car ferry loading platform. During a storm in 1926, the Atlantus broke free from its mooring and came to rest at Sunset Beach. Despite attempts to move her, she remains at this spot and millions of tourists have come to see her slowly sink into the sand. Sunset Beach is also where Cape May diamonds are easily found. This beach is reached by taking the Garden State Parkway south to the last exit.   Then go straight over the bridge and take Lafayette Street south; make a right turn onto Route 606 west, also called Sunset Boulevard.   Proceed straight to Sunset Beach.

Cape May is famous for clear quartz crystals known as Cape May diamonds.   The source of these "diamonds" is 200 miles up the Delaware River, where swift currents erode away pockets of quartz.   It takes the crystals thousands of years to journey to Cape May. When they reach the mouth of the Delaware Bay, the tumbled smooth crystals are caught in the strong flow of water in the bay.   This flow of water constantly hits the concrete Atlantus, swirling stones, pebbles, and diamonds onto Sunset Beach.   Cape May diamonds are found from the rock pile just south of the ship to about two to three miles north, up the beach.   During the winter months when the surf is rougher, larger stones come ashore.   The most productive diamond hunting is after a storm with northwest winds.   Plan your trip to Cape May in the fall, winter, or spring, avoiding the height of the tourist season.

The best time to find diamonds is during a receding tide.   As the tide retreats, small waves wash over the many stones found along the water's edge and the diamonds glisten in the sunlight.   To find diamonds in the piles of stone not being washed by the waves, gently move your hand across the top of the stones.   Focus only on the area immediately in front of you.   Trying to look everywhere at once will result in fewer finds.   Cape May diamonds range in size from as small as a grain of sand, to as large as a chicken egg.

The Kechemeche Indians were the first to find the clear quartz stones.   They believed the stones had supernatural powers, bringing success and good fortune to the possessor. Bonds of friendship and good will were supported by the gift or exchange of the sacred gems.

Rock and mineral enthusiasts enjoy polishing the Cape May diamonds. They use an electric powered machine called a "tumbler." When the stones have been polished and cut, they have the appearance of genuine diamonds. Processed Cape May diamonds make beautiful jewelry pieces when mounted in gold or silver. Other quartz stones commonly found on Sunset Beach include citrine quartz (clear yellow to red-purple or orange quartz,) smoky quartz (pale brown to black quartz,) and rose quartz (pink or rose-red quartz.) These stones can also be polished and made into jewelry.

Other beach collectibles found on Sunset Beach include rocks containing fossils. Rarer finds include sharks' teeth and Indian arrowheads.

Other New Jersey Beach Collectibles

Skate egg cases, called "Devil's Purse," are frequently found on New Jersey's beaches. These black egg cases from the common skate are rectangular with curled horn-shaped extensions at each corner. They were once anchored in the subtidal zone, became detached, and washed onto the beach. They are often a mystery to beach strollers.

Another beach collectible you can find on the Jersey Shore, especially in the area of rock jetties, is "sea glass," also known as "beach glass." When beach strolling, look through the shells and stones. You will come across frosted pieces of colored glass. The glass is usually from broken bottles and jars. It has been worn down by the action of the sea and sand into translucent brown, yellowish green, dark green, royal blue, aquamarine, and white pieces of sea glass. Red is a rare find, perhaps from boat lights. We have found several frosted light blue bottle stoppers, another rare find. Sometimes a piece of sea glass is identifiable by the design or writing on the glass. Finding a piece of glass from the container of a product packaged decades ago, is very exciting. After collecting the many different sizes, shapes, and colors of sea glass, display your treasures in decorative clear glass containers. The beautiful colors and shapes blend with any decor.

Sea glass, Cape May diamonds, moon snails, jingle shells, and jackknife clams are just some of the wonderful finds at the Jersey Shore. Come spend some time at the places mentioned and see what exciting discoveries you can make. To avoid the crowds, before Memorial Day or after Labor Day will be the best time to visit. Remember, there are 127 miles of beach, so pack the map and visit other beaches, too.

8

Cape Cod, Massachusetts

Cape Cod is a peninsula jutting out into the Atlantic Ocean off the southeastern portion of Massachusetts. The scenic Cape Cod Canal flows between Cape Cod and the mainland. From here, the peninsula extends east about thirty-five miles and then north about thirty miles. The cape is approximately twelve miles across at its widest and a mile wide at its narrowest. This peninsula is a glacial deposit continuously being changed by wind and the movement of water. The sandy shoreline is washing away in some areas while building up in other areas. In 1961, the Cape Cod National Seashore was established by the National Park Service to help protect this natural resource. The National Seashore encompasses forty miles of coastline, including a 27,000 acre section from Chatham to Provincetown.

Cape Cod lures vacationers with a refreshing seashore environment consisting of roadside vistas, flowering fields, weathered gable-roofed houses, beautiful wide beaches, and picturesque harbors. Visitors can take part in activities including fishing, whale watching, golfing, shopping, swimming, sunbathing, hiking, bird watching, bicycling, and shelling.

Shelling on Cape Cod

Cape Cod offers shelling on Atlantic Ocean beaches and the beaches of Cape Cod Bay. A variety of shell species can be found on both. If you are interested in taking edible shellfish, be advised town licenses are required. Regulations and fees vary from town to town.

Shells commonly found on Cape Cod:

False Angel Wing   Soft-shell Clam
Common Jingle Shell   Eastern Oyster
Northern Horse Mussel   Blue Mussel
Atlantic Surf Clam   Blood Ark
Purplish Tagelus   Northern Quahog
Arctic Wedge Clam   Atlantic Bay Scallop
Channeled Whelk   Gould's Pandora
Amethyst Gem Clam   Lunar Dove Shell
Stout Razor Clam   Knobbed Whelk
Well-ribbed Dove Shell   Transverse Ark
Atlantic Jackknife Clam   Thick-lipped Drill
Common Sand Dollar
Solitary Paper Bubble
Common Northern Moon Shell
Common Atlantic Slipper Shell
New England Whelk (Massachusetts' State Shell)

Sand Dollars at South Beach, Chatham

Chatham is located mid-Cape at the "elbow" of the peninsula. At Chatham Light, one of the five lighthouses located on Cape Cod, there is a beautiful Atlantic Ocean overlook. From here you see the National Seashore's North Beach to the left and South Beach to the right. On February 2, 1987, a violent winter storm struck the area. The barrier beach known as Nauset Peninsula was breached. This resulted in South Beach. An island immediately after the "break," South Beach has become attached to the mainland and is now a peninsula. The continuing movement of sand is extending this peninsula southward. Conveniently, this barrier beach is now accessible by foot. Before the break the beach was reached by boat.

Parking is very limited at the beaches in Chatham. It is suggested you walk from your lodging to access the beach at the Chatham Lighthouse. Walk to the water and then go to the right. You will be walking south on South Beach. The beach is approximately four miles long. A walk to the south point took us about two hours, not including shelling time. Wearing shoes is recommended when shelling here and on all Cape Cod beaches, as the sand is very coarse. A walk down and back on South Beach without wearing shoes will likely result in painful blisters.

The main shelling method used on South Beach is beach strolling. Shells can be found in the shallow water and on the sand. Be sure to search in the seaweed at the high tide line for many varieties of shells. They can be found all along the walk to the end of the peninsula. Many of the species listed above may be found. In contrast to the clams, jingle shells, jackknife clams, and scallop shells found south of the New England States, the shells found here are generally larger and thicker.

Interesting collectibles found on South Beach are "cobbles." These attractive stones vary in color, size, and texture. Their color combinations include black and white; orange, beige, and green; light green and dark green; gray and white; light pink and dark gray; pink and burgundy; white marbled with burgundy and gray; and green, dark red, and orange. The solid-colored cobbles are white, light green, gray, brick red, tan, yellow, and brown. Cobblestones found on South Beach are the size of chicken eggs and smaller. The cobbles are also called "tracer stones." Geologists can trace the cobbles back to their originating rock source. Many of the sources are hundreds of miles away from Cape Cod.

On the South Beach walk, numerous Atlantic Bay Scallops can be found. They vary in color and range in size from one and one-half inches to four inches long. The scallops are dark gray, light gray, brown, and orange. They are also found with combinations of dark brown and beige, gray and beige, orange and white. Sometimes their colors are rayed. Unlike the Calico Scallop shell, the Atlantic Bay Scallop shell is thinner and lighter in weight. The Atlantic Bay Scallop is a very popular seafood. The scallop's single one and one-half inch muscle is the edible part.

Another collectible abundant on the beach here is the sea star. On one spring trip we found many sea stars, each about a half-inch across, scattered along the high tide line. The sun and wind had naturally dried them. We were also pleased to find a piece of "crumb of bread sponge." This sponge is yellowish-green and grows twelve inches wide and two inches high. It has a thin crust, texture like breadcrumbs, and pores resembling volcanoes. Immediately upon seeing it, we thought it was a piece of plastic foam on the otherwise litter-free beach. We were surprised it was a species of sponge.

Cape Cod is a popular spot for finding "true" sand dollars. Their range, however, is from Labrador to Maryland. If you remember from chapter four, most people refer to Keyhole Urchins as sand dollars. Keyhole Urchins have keyhole-shaped holes in their shell, or test. Common Sand Dollars are circular and have a design resembling a spoke-like arrangement of five petals similar to Keyhole Urchins. They also have fine velvety spines covering their shell. However, Common Sand Dollars do not have holes through their shells.

When strolling South Beach, look for sand dollars in the intertidal zone as the tide goes out. They are often found on top of the sand with their convex side facing upward. The most productive sand dollar hunting area we experienced here was about two miles down South Beach, or about halfway to the end of the peninsula. We found twelve sand dollars on one excursion. About four hours after high tide, the retreating water had left the sand dollars on the beach. Many sandbars were exposed and sand dollars were found on them also. All the Common Sand Dollars (illustration 26) were the spineless, bleached white remains of the animal.

We had walked alone on the beach for about three miles when we suddenly had the distinct feeling we were being followed. We turned to look behind us and to our surprise we saw a seal in the water. When it noticed us watching, the seal began showing off by arching out of the water. It continued to follow us down the beach, appearing to be as inquisitive about us as we were about him. On another trip, there were about fifty seals frol-

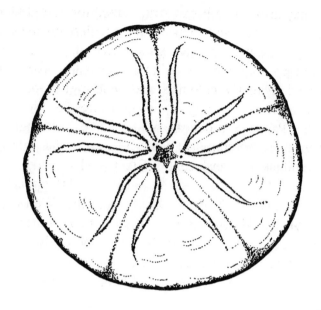

illustration 26   Common Sand Dollar

icking just off shore.   Other wildlife we observed included a hawk enjoying lunch and four young red fox
playing.

When walking back from the south end of South
Beach, walk on the bay side.   Here you will find species
of shells less likely to be found on the ocean side.
Mussels, Atlantic Jackknife Clams, Northern Quahogs,
and other varieties of clams can be found on the mud
flats at low tide.   It is also likely you will be able to
observe these mollusks alive in their habitat.

Cape Cod has many miles of shoreline along
Buzzards Bay, Nantucket Sound, Cape Cod Bay, and the
Atlantic Ocean.   This offers many opportunities for
shelling and searching for other beach collectibles.   We
suggest exploring the bays.   Perhaps you will find a
Transverse Ark, the most common ark of the bay shore.

You may also find a Blood Ark, named for its red blood, rare among mollusks. One of the smallest bivalves, the Amethyst Gem Clam can also be found. These one-eighth inch purple and white triangular valves were once collected by early colonists and sent to Europe to be embroidered on clothing. Another interesting find is the Gould's Pandora, a delicate, flat bivalve, seemingly too thin to house an animal. When held up to the light, the live mollusk is translucent. Other shells found at the bays include the Lunar Dove Shell, the Solitary Paper Bubble, the Thick-lipped Drill, and the Well-ribbed Dove Shell. Massachusetts is the northern end of these shells' range. Obviously, a visit to Cape Cod will keep a sheller happily occupied for many hours.

9

Down East Maine

Maine is the northernmost state on the East Coast and the closest point in the United States to the European continent. It encompasses a landmass of 33,215 square miles. Nicknamed the "Pine Tree State" for its seventeen million forested acres, Maine also includes 6,000 lakes and ponds, 32,000 miles of rivers and streams, 2,000 islands, and 3,478 miles of coastline. A term synonymous with coastal Maine is "Down East." Eighteenth and nineteenth century sailors created the expression. Sailing their schooners from Boston to Maine, they traveled in an easterly direction with the wind at their backs, or down wind.

To really experience Down East, begin by taking U.S. Route 1, the coastal route. It is a scenic drive beginning at the southern tip of Maine and continuing east along the coast. To explore all the nooks and crannies of the coast, you must turn off the highway and take roads leading to the water. A good road map is essential. Use the map to help you locate coves and peninsulas. Around the many coves is where you will find the small towns and fishing villages. When stopping for meals or shopping, talk to the local merchants and residents. They can direct you to spectacular views, hiking trails, and beaches not generally advertised or identified on maps.

The Southcoast Region of Maine is referred to as the "Gateway to Maine." Here is where the state's magnificent coast begins. Along Maine's coastline the Atlantic Ocean washes around peninsulas and flows into peaceful harbors, laps onto sandy beaches, and thunders against rocky cliffs. To put the size of the coastline into perspective, it is the same length as California's coastline, but Maine's is laid out in only 250 air miles. In the Southcoast region the beaches consist of long stretches of fine white sand. The most popular beaches are York, Ogunquit, Wells, Portland, Old Orchard Beach, and the Kennebunks. State parks in this region with popular beaches include Reid State Park, Popham Beach State Park, and Crescent Beach State Park. All of Maine's beaches are excellent for walking, sunning, and shelling. However, most people do not like to swim at Maine's beaches because the summer water temperature ranges from only fifty-four to fifty-nine degrees.

The Down East/Acadia Region comprises all of Hancock and the southern and central portions of Penobscot counties. Here the coastline is more rugged and the peninsulas jut out far into the Atlantic. Acadia National Park is an excellent example of this beauty.

The Sunrise Coast is the last stretch of Down East Maine. It has one thousand miles of rugged coastline and is the nation's easternmost land. The Sunrise Coast has dense woods, alive with many species of animals and approximately 200,000 acres of open land where wild blueberries are raised and harvested. In July the blueberries begin to ripen and the hills take on a blue hue.

Along the coastline, rocky cliffs and pine trees overlook the many harbors dotted with lobstermen's boats and many sailboats.

It is important to exercise extreme caution when exploring the Maine coast. When hiking, you must be sure rocky ground is secure. Use good judgement when walking along rock cliffs and avoid wet slippery rocks. Also, be very aware of the changing tide, especially from low to high. The tides in northern Maine are the highest in the continental United States and range from approximately twelve to twenty feet, increasing as you travel east. The rapid flow of water during tide changes is awesome to see, but at the same time can be dangerous. At low tide you may be able to walk across exposed stone beds to islands. Should the tide start to come in, you will be stranded until the next tide change. Tide tables are available at Maine State Information Centers and in local newspapers. The tide tables provide you with the exact time of high and low tide. The benefit of an extreme low tide when shelling is the vast amount of intertidal zone exposed. This provides a large area for collecting shells and observing marine life.

When shelling on the coast of Maine, you will experience many aspects of nature. A variety of birds, including bald eagles, soar overhead. Other wildlife frequently seen include porcupine foraging for food, seals passing by in the rushing tide, chipmunks scurrying about, and deer hiding in the brush. You might even have the opportunity to see bobcat, mink, beaver, and moose.

The weather on Maine's coast can change quickly. Be prepared for temperature changes by bringing extra clothing to layer on and take off as needed. Also, be prepared for damp and wet weather by packing appropriate foul weather gear. Fog along Maine's coast is very common. It might stay around for several days, clear up in a matter of minutes, or be non-existent around the next bend in the road. Fog can create beautiful views or make roads, forests, and mountains seem to disappear. However, fog will never hide the seashells.

Shelling in "Down East" Maine

When we tell someone we are taking a trip to Maine, a common response is, "I guess this isn't a shelling vacation." We then help correct their misconception. The coast of Maine is abundant with easily observable sea life, shells, and other fascinating beach collectibles. The state's irregular and deeply sheltered coastline, coupled with a limited number of sandy beaches, provides a variety of shell hunting environments. Where sand beaches exist, the sand colors include white, chestnut brown, brick red, black, and tan accented with other subtle colors. Most of the sand originated from glacial deposits. Only a small amount of new sand is deposited by rivers and streams. Approximately sixty-five miles of Maine's coast is sandy beach, but this is less than two percent of the total. The remaining ninety-eight percent is jagged bedrock, boulders, and cobbles.

The shelling locations (map 4) discussed in this chapter, traveling from west to east, are Sand Beach at Acadia National Park, Mt. Desert Island; Schoodic Peninsula, Acadia National Park, Winter Harbor; Petit Manan National Wildlife Refuge, Stuben; Sandy Beach, Jonesport; Jasper Beach, Machiasport; West Quoddy Head State Park, Lubec; and beaches in Perry.

Shells Commonly Found in Down East Maine

Northern Horse Mussel	Atlantic Plate Limpet
Blue Mussel	Common Periwinkle
Atlantic Deep-sea Scallop	Iceland Scallop
Eastern Mud Whelk	Common Sand Dollar
Atlantic Dogwinkle	Soft-shell Clam
Atlantic Jackknife Clam	Green Sea Urchin
Northern Rough Periwinkle	
Common Northern Whelk	
Common Atlantic Slipper Shell	
New England Whelk	

(also called New England Neptune)

Sand Beach at Acadia National Park, Mount Desert Island

Mount Desert Island, the third largest island on America's East Coast, is located just off the coast approximately nine miles from Ellsworth. Traveling on Route 1, take Route 3 East from Ellsworth. After crossing the Mount Desert Narrows, the Thompson Island Information Center will be on the right. Continue on Route 3 for approximately eight more miles. You will see the Acadia Park entrance sign on the right. Turn here and stop at the Hulls Cove Information Center. At the information center you should pick up a free Acadia Park Visitors' Guide, review the park regulations, look at area maps, view the introductory film, and talk to the park guides to acquaint yourself with the park.

Acadia National Park is the oldest national park east of the Mississippi River and the only coastal national park north of Florida. The park's more than 40,000 acres includes the famous 1,530 foot Cadillac Mountain, the

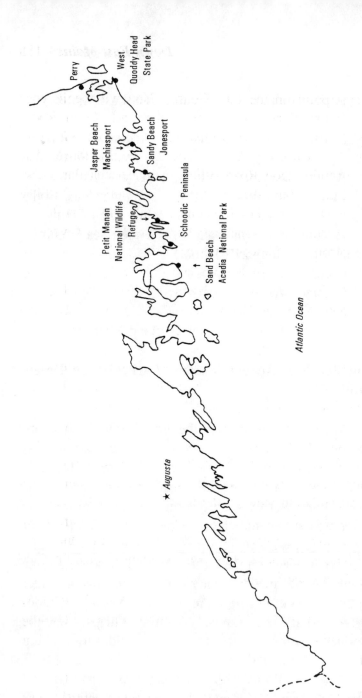

map 4 Down East Maine

highest point on the East Coast. You will begin your Acadia experience by traveling the Park Loop Road. Purchase the *Acadia National Park Motorists' Guide* to enhance your enjoyment of this self-guided tour. The twenty-mile Loop Road offers many spectacular views including Jordan Pond, Frenchman's Overlook, Cadillac Mountain, Bubble Pond, Thunder Hole, and Sand Beach.

Acadia Park is basically rock-bound. However, ten miles from the Newport Cove Visitor's Center you will find the park's only sand beach on the ocean, sensibly named "Sand Beach." At Sand Beach you can hike on nearby paths, sit and enjoy the sun and scenery, attempt a swim in the brisk ocean, and do some observational shelling.

One very interesting feature to observe here is the sand. Consisting of very few mineral particles, the sand is basically the crushed shells of mussels, clams, and sea urchins. Close examination will also reveal many pieces of urchin spines.

When you leave Sand Beach, continue your drive along the park road. Look back at Sand Beach and enjoy the magnificent view of the beach, rocky cliffs, and the surrounding forest. As you proceed along the Park Loop Road, stop and explore the many rock ledges, mud flats, and bolder beaches. Here you can identify many marine life and seashell species.

Mussel Beds at Acadia National Park, Schoodic Peninsula

Schoodic Peninsula is located approximately nineteen miles from Ellsworth. Traveling on Route 1 north, turn off Route 1 onto Route 186. The entrance to the 2,080 acre Schoodic section of Acadia National Park is in the

town of Winter Harbor. After entering the park, you will
drive a short distance before coming to a one-way sign.
Just before this sign, turn right into the Frazier's Point
picnic area.

Frazier's Point is the first of several observational
shelling locations on Schoodic Peninsula. Be sure to bring
your camera. Here you can look for shells along the
pebble beach to the right of the dock and around the rock
ledges to the left of the dock. In the intertidal zone, plant
and animal life is ever changing. Each tide rearranges the
rocks, shells, sand, sea creatures, and vegetation. The best
time to observe this environment is when the tide is at its
lowest.

At Frazier's Point, periwinkles, limpets, sea urchins,
sand dollars, barnacles, and large three-inch Blue Mussels
are common. The Blue Mussels are black and blue on the
outside and silver inside. They have a brown periostracum. Mussels are oblong and fan shaped. Their hinge
is near or at the narrower front end. Beds of Blue Mussels
live and grow clustered around the base of the rocks in the
intertidal zone, their larger end protruding from the mud.
They are anchored to stone, rocks, or pilings by a
"byssus," a tough filament. At Frazier's Point during low
tide, you can observe live mussels. On the left side of the
dock among the mussel beds, you are likely to see
Common Sand Dollars washed onto shore or half buried in
the mud. These sand dollars lack spines and have been
cleaned by the motion of the water and bleached by the
sun.

Barnacles (illustration 27) are another interesting find
at Frazier's Point. They are usually seen at low tide on
pilings, other shells, and rocks. Barnacles are sedentary
crustaceans. Their interlocking limy shells form a cone
shape. These shells, also known as plates, close at low

illustration 27   Barnacles on a shell

tide preventing the animal from drying out. The plates open at high tide allowing the crustacean to feed on plankton by means of extended cilia. Barnacles were named in ancient times when it was believed the limy shells enclosed the embryo of the Barnacle Duck and the cilia were the duck's future feathers.

Also found at Frasier's Point are dead sea urchins left behind by the receding tide. The meat inside will be a feast for small bugs searching for food or for the always hungry sea gulls. It is interesting to watch the sea gulls flying overhead with sea urchins between their beaks. They drop the urchins in the parking lot or on the rocks to break them open. They then enjoy their meal.

The urchins found in Maine are Green Sea Urchins (illustration 28.) They grow to about three and one-quarter inches wide and one and one-half inches high. Some of the sea urchins found are empty shells bleached by the sun, and others are meat-filled with spines still in-

illustration 28   The Shell or Test of the Green Sea Urchin

tact. Interestingly, sea urchins are a relative of sea stars. This relationship seems unusual until you look inside a sea urchin. Although oval, the urchin has the radial symmetry or five-rayed pattern of the sea star and its other relative the sand dollar. The sea urchin's test is composed of many small pieces of shells positioned edge to edge, forming an external covering of the flesh. The shell is supported in the center by bones leaning on each other in a pyramid arrangement. Moveable spines protect the sea urchin from predators. Urchins live underwater from the low tide line to deeper water and in underwater rock crevices where they avoid light.

After enjoying Frazier's Point, continue on the one-way park road. You will see rugged shoreline on the right and dense forest on the left. You can stop at the many turnouts and view magnificent seascapes, small coves, rock islands, lighthouses in the distance, working lobster boats, and the mountains of Mount Desert Island. At several locations you will be able to park on the side of the road, get out of your car, and enjoy the scenery and fresh salt air. Observational shelling opportunities exist at the many coves where the sea crashes against the piles of beach rock. Under and around the rocks you will find many of the species of shells found in Maine. On the granite and basalt ledges you can often see the sea urchin shells left behind by the gulls.

Beach Collectibles at Petit Manan National Wildlife Refuge

Petit Manan National Wildlife Refuge is a coastal complex consisting of 3,335 acres. The largest section is Petit Manan Point, Steuben, containing 1,991 acres. Here you will be able to enjoy a spectacular beach hike. Traveling on Route 1 north, make a right turn onto Pigeon Hill Road. Take this road for about six miles. At the refuge entrance there is a small gravel parking lot. Here there is a bulletin board with information about the area and a map indicating two hiking trails. After reading the information board, drive another half mile to the parking area for the shore hike.

The hike to the shore is the "John Hollingswood Memorial Trail." This coastal footpath is a tribute to John Hollingswood who devoted ten years to photographing the beauty of the Refuge System. Wearing hiking boots is recommended. The trail winds through a small blueberry barren, a spruce and mixed hardwood forest, jack pine stands, cedar swamp, and fresh water marsh. It then opens onto a rock strewn beach. The trail turns to the left along the rocky shoreline. The stretch of beach to your right is along a small cove named Cable Cove. Go out onto the beach and explore this area. From the beach the trail swings back into the woods and returns to the parking area. This hike is 1.5 miles roundtrip and is considered primitive, with rocky terrain and exposed roots.

For a longer hike along the water, we recommend going to the right where the trail takes you out onto the rocky beach. Continue walking along the shore. You will have to climb over a large granite ledge to get to the next cove. The majority of the hike will be on cobblestone beaches and rock ledges. It is definitely not a sand beach stroll. You will be completely awed by the beautiful Maine coast scenery and your excitement will push you onward. This extended area of the hike is not a loop trail so be prepared to hike back.

Shells seen on the Shore Trail hike include sea urchins, mussels, limpets, and periwinkles. The sea urchins and mussels are most often found at the high water line and Common Periwinkles (illustration 29) are found piled up among the cobbles and larger rocks. The beach on one of the coves is mostly made up of periwinkles. Live periwinkles can be observed in pools of water on the rock ledges. One of the coves has so many sun-bleached mussels its shoreline appears light blue. Other likely finds on the Shore Trail hike are the shed shells of the Jonah Crab and Atlantic Rock Crab. These shells have beautiful red and cream color designs.

Beach collectibles you are likely to find at Petit Manan include lobster pots and lobster pot markers. They are washed ashore by strong ocean currents, especially

illustration 29 Common Periwinkles

storm currents. Fun to collect, these items are often used to decorate seashore homes. After you hike past several coves and past the stand of pine trees, the coast curves to the right and the Petit Manan Island Lighthouse is visible offshore. Here you should find several lobster pots and lobster pot markers. As you beachcomb, you will hear the "hummmm" of working boats as the lobstermen haul in their catch of fresh Maine lobster. Note that a shelling hike to this area of the beach and back to your car could take four to five hours.

Whether you choose to explore the first couple of coves or hike to the end of the point, you are likely to experience and observe many interesting aspects of nature. Along with what is mentioned above, we have found a large wooden oar and a note in a bottle from a person who lives in Texas. Additionally, we have had the opportunity to observe deer, bald eagles, mink, and porcupine living in this refuge.

White Sand at Sandy Beach

Sandy Beach is located on Chandler Bay in Jonesport. When traveling north on Route 1, take the second Route 187 road towards Jonesport for seven and one-half miles. Look for a white sign on the left advertising "Church Enterprises General Contractor." Keep in mind this sign may not always be there. (You will have driven too far if you have gone more than seven and one-half miles from Route 1, and you see several houses just to the left of the road, overlooking the water.) At the white sign, turn left down the gravel road. Drive about 100 feet and parallel park on the right side of the road. There is room for about five or six cars. Then walk down the path through the pine trees and sand dunes to the beautiful crescent-shaped white sand beach.

This beach is one of the few white sand beaches in "Down East" Maine. It also has another rarity for Maine, sand dunes. Upon close inspection, the sand here is mostly white with black, brown, and tan pieces of shells and minerals. Shells commonly found on Sandy Beach include the Common Atlantic Slipper Shell, Atlantic Jackknife Clam, New England Neptune, Northern Horse Mussel, and Common Northern Whelk. Other beach collectibles found on Sandy Beach include barnacles, egg cases of the Common Northern Whelk, and driftwood worn by the surf and bleached by the sun. We have even found the skull of a cow on this beach, so far our most unexpected beach find.

Shelling is best at Sandy Beach when the tide is low. In the intertidal zone, especially after a storm, the beach is littered with collectibles. Often, most of the beach is covered with a thick carpet of yellowish-brown rockweed, kelp, and other varieties of what is generalized as seaweed. Many of the larger pieces of kelp wash ashore with their holdfasts still attached to Northern Horse Mussels. Search through the seaweed and treasures will be found.

Jasper Stones on Jasper Beach

Jasper Beach is located on a peninsula in Machiasport. The ride to Jasper Beach is a scenic drive along the Machias Bay. From the center of Machias, travel on Route 1 north to Route 92. Jasper Beach is located about nine and one-half miles down Route 92. You will see a sign on the left side of the road identifying this eleven acre park. Enter here and travel a short distance on the dirt road. Park at the pile of stones.

Jasper Beach is a stone beach forming a half-mile crescent around Howard's Cove on Machias Bay. Sloping down to the water on either side of the cove are rock cliffs covered with forest. The ocean's waves have built up a beach consisting of jasper and volcanic rhyolite. These wave-tumbled and polished pebbles and rocks, with their extremely smooth finish, make up almost the entire beach. At low tide you may be able to see some chestnut brown sand at the water's edge. At the low water line the beach consists of marble-size pebbles. The stones gradually increase in size up the beach until they are about the size of softballs at the farthest point away from the water.

Rhyolite and jasper give the beach its unusual tint. Rhyolite is a very acid volcanic rock, the lava form of granite. Jasper is an opaque, red, green, brown, or yellow cryptocrystalline quartz. Some of the stones contain combinations of two or more colors of jasper. Each stone is mostly one color with thin stripes of another.

Seashells can be found on Jasper Beach near the rock cliffs and include Atlantic Deep-sea Scallops, Blue Mussels, Soft-shell Clams, and all the species of periwinkles found in Maine. The most productive shelling may be at the left side of the cove. Just stroll the beach and look in between the stones for shells.

The Sand at Perry and "Quoddy"

In addition to tan sand from Sand Beach at Acadia National Park, white sand from Sandy Beach at Jonesport, and chestnut brown sand from Jasper Beach at Machiasport, you can find red and black sand at the easternmost part of Maine.

Red sand is found at Perry, a town located halfway between the Equator and the North Pole on the 45th parallel. On Route 1 there is a red granite stone marking the exact location of this halfway point. The view from Route 1 in Perry offers nothing more than forest. Take the shore road, and you will see beautiful panoramic views of the Passamaquoddy Bay and the Canadian Islands.

Traveling on Route 1, take route 190 for 2.7 miles. On the left you will see a crescent-shaped beach to explore. Gleason's Cove, a state operated park, is another good beach to investigate. The sand at Perry is a deep red consisting of red granite. Its texture is very coarse.

Black sand can be found at the 400 acre West Quoddy Head State Park, Lubec. Traveling on Route 1, take Route 189 east, and follow the signs to the park. The sand here is coarse, made up of black volcanic rock. Its texture is much like the sand at Perry, consisting of very small rock fragments and finer rock granules. West Quoddy Head State Park sits on rock cliffs ninety to two hundred feet high and is the easternmost point of the continental United States. From the park's cliffs, visitors can view the smashing surf and Canada's Grand Manan Island. This park is also well known for its red and white striped lighthouse.

Down East Maine offers visitors many varied shelling environments. The beaches are filled with interesting treasures; the beautiful scenery, abundant wildlife, and crisp salt air beckon you to return here again and again.

PART THREE:
YOUR SHELLS AS SOUVENIRS

10

Proper Handling of Shells

The proper handling of shells must begin the moment you pick them up off the sand or scoop them out of the water. This is especially important with fragile shells such as Keyhole Urchins, Angel Wings, Cabrit's Murex, and Common Jingle Shells. These shells may not make the trip safely off the beach unless you handle them with care and transport them properly. The more durable shells such as Florida Fighting Conch, Florida Horse Conch, whelk, olive, and cone shells can withstand some rough travel.

Transporting Shells

Before arriving at the beach for a day of shelling, formulate a plan and gather together the supplies you will need to carry your "finds" safely off the beach. Required supplies will include a sturdy ten-gallon plastic bag, a plastic net fruit bag, and a knapsack for carrying big durable shells. Also required is a one-gallon size plastic bag for medium size shells, a sandwich size bag for small shells, and a small pail or other plastic container for fragile shells. Pack shells according to size to prevent heavier shells from breaking smaller, more delicate ones. Lay or stack fragile shells carefully and do not bump or shake the container.

Once off the beach and back at your lodging, unpack the shells, let them dry, and then repack them for transport home. When repacking your shells, take the time to wrap the fragile ones in tissue paper or paper towels. Then carefully layer them in an empty tissue box or a small plastic container. This will help protect them from breaking. Important–very delicate or special shells should be packed individually.

Cleaning Shells

Many shells found on the beach have been cleaned naturally by rolling around in the surf. The animal has died or been eaten and only the shell is left. These are the shells you can pack for transport without cleaning. Other shells will have part of the dead, decaying animal in the shell. Your sense of smell will quickly identify them. Other shells may have the live animal inside. If you collect these shells, obey the local live shelling laws.

Many methods are used to clean shells. The simpler methods include boiling, freezing, or soaking them in rubbing alcohol. Other methods require using formalin, lye, acid, and bacteria and should only be used by professionals. Used improperly, these cleaning methods can damage your shells.

Boiling is fast, convenient, and the most widely used method of removing the animal or any plant life from the shell. The length of time you boil the shell depends on its size. Boiling time for smaller shells requires one to three minutes while larger shells require five to eight minutes. Boiling shells for too long removes the natural oils and will destroy their luster. It is best to place the shells into room temperature water first, then gradually bring the water to a boil. After boiling the shell and letting it cool, carefully remove the animal with a nut pick, a pair of tweezers, or a sewing needle. Pull gently and slowly so the animal does not break off inside the shell. After the animal is removed, soak the shell in a solution of bleach (30%) and water (70%) to remove any remaining material. Also, if the periostracum is still intact, the bleach solution will remove it. Note, do not bleach Florida Fighting Conch, olives, or cowries. The bleach may severely dull the colors of these shells. When using a bleach solution, always clean one shell of each species to test the outcome. After completing the cleaning process, rinse the shells with clean water. If barnacles, coral, or other shells still must be removed, carefully scrape them off the shell with a small knife or nut pick.

Another method used for removing the animal is to freeze the specimen. After freezing it for about seventy-two hours, you can remove the animal. You can also soak the shell in rubbing alcohol for about seventy-two hours and then remove the animal. Using rubbing alcohol is the best method for small shells less than one inch in size, as it should not damage them.

After cleaning the shells, you can apply mineral oil to the outside of the shells to restore their luster. Never apply lacquer to your shells if you want to keep their natural quality. However, if you want a low grade shell to look good for use on a craft project, lacquer will do the trick.

152 The ART of SHELLING

To clean sand dollars and Keyhole Urchins, soak them in a solution of bleach (50%) and water (50%) until they turn white. If necessary, gently scrub the test with a soft toothbrush. Do not leave them in the bleach solution any longer than necessary. If they are left in the solution too long, they will become even more fragile. After the bleaching process is completed, rinse the sand dollars and Keyhole Urchins in fresh water and put them on paper towels in the sun to dry. To make urchins more durable, paint them with a coat of water base white glue. The glue soaks into the urchins and dries hard and clear. There is a similar "sand dollar hardener" product sometimes available in variety stores and craft shops.

To clean sea urchins, soak them in a bleach (50%) and water (50%) solution. Take them out of the solution when their spines fall off and the meat is cleaned out from the shell. Do not leave the urchins in the solution any longer than necessary or they will break apart. Green Sea Urchins will bleach white, or they will be a light green. Some may even have purple or green stripes. When you take the urchins out of the solution, rinse them in clean water and put them on paper towels to dry.

Searching for and finding shells and other beach collectibles is the exciting and fun part of shelling. However, the proper handling of your finds is the most important if you want to enjoy them and share them with others.

11

The Many Uses of Shells

Seashells begin as the supporting structures of mollusks. When the animal dies and the shells become empty, they turn into prized gifts for mankind–gifts to be searched for, contemplated, and shared with others. This fascination with one of nature's more beautiful creations is well documented.

A Historical Perspective

Since man has been around, he has been collecting seashells. Archeologists find shells all over the world, many in sites dating back over 15,000 years. On several occasions shells have been found in parts of the world far from where they naturally occur. A Pacific shell was discovered in the ruins of a Swiss village and an Atlantic shell was found in an Etruscan grave. Shells from France were found with the remains of Emperor Caligula in Rome. The ashes of Pompeii included shells from an ancient Mediterranean collection, to include a cone shell from as far away as the Indian Ocean.

Native American societies used seashells for many purposes. Out of necessity each society was self-sustaining, with their own language and divergent views. The tribes were also separated by many weeks of travel time. Despite their differences, complex routes and methods of communication and exchange linked these communities. The discoveries of shells and sharks' teeth from the Gulf of Mexico, found across the eastern part of the country, are evidence of this. These shells and sharks' teeth had been transformed into beautiful works of art. The Onondagas, the most centrally located of the five Iroquois tribes, became the "wampum keepers." It was an Iroquois custom to accompany all important statements with a gift to ensure the statement was true. Wampum became the customary gift. White wampum was made from the central column of the whelk shell and the more valuable purple wampum was made from the hard-shell quahog clam. Indian societies used shells for other purposes including jewelry, clothing decoration, and utensils. The surface of large conch shells was inscribed with sacred images and these shells were used as drinking cups.

Throughout history shells have been made into musical instruments, tools, or as artifacts in religious rituals. Other ancient societies used shells for currency. Today, where found in abundance, oyster and clam shells are crushed and used to make driveways and highway and railroad beds. Ground clam shells are added to chicken feed to promote eggshell development. Several varieties of shells are used to make jewelry. Helmet and conch shells are carved into cameos and small shells are simply strung together to make necklaces.

Man has used shells for religious and mythological

symbolism for centuries.   He has also used them to inspire art and architectural design.   Mollusks build their shell with varied and intricate beauty.   They instinctively incorporate complex mathematical formulas to create their functional architecture.   The architectural curve of seashells is a "magic ratio" recurring throughout art and nature.   The magical number is .618034.   In 1202, Leonardo Fibonacci discovered a mysterious series of numbers that is significant in art, architecture, ocean-ography, botany, biology, astronomy, and music.   Each number in the series is the sum of the two preceding numbers.   The numbers 1, 2, 3, 5, 8, 13, 21, 34, 55, 89, 144, 233... and the 100th number in the series, 354,224,848,179,261,915,075, are as precise as nature. If you divide a Fibonacci number by the next highest number, you will find it is precisely .618034 times as large as the number that follows.   This works for all numbers beyond the 14th in the sequence.   The proportion of .618034 to 1 is called "the golden mean." Plankton and shellfish of the earliest forms exhibit this logarithmic spiral.   The proportion is also the mathematical basis for the shape of Greek vases, the Parthenon, playing cards, sunflowers, the great galaxies of outer space, and snail shells. The Greeks' art and architecture was based on the golden mean.   They probably did not understand the mathematical basis, but they realized the shape was very pleasing to behold.

One of the most spectacularly proportioned sea spirals is the beautiful chambered nautilus.   As the animal grows, it builds larger and larger compartments, forming an expanding spiral.   When each new compartment is completed, the mollusk crawls forward, closing off the vacated compartment with a layer of mother-of-pearl.   This traps air and gas in the previous living quarters, allowing the structure to remain buoyant even with its massive size.

One species of murex became historically signif-icant in the fifteenth century B.C. The people of Sidon and Tyre found a way to extract a purple dye from the mollusk. This dye making process was kept a secret for a long time. The dye was used to color the robes of Roman and Byzantine emperors. The robes' rich hues were very impressive. Cloth the color of blood and in shades of purple, magenta, and scarlet have been found in royal tombs. The rare materials were expensive; however, they were in demand throughout the ancient world.

At the end of the 15th century, Columbus landed in the Americas. Objects brought from the New World included seashells. The wealthy quickly became inter-ested in collecting these treasures. They not only enjoyed the beauty of the shell, but their desire to learn more about the animal that inhabited it increased. It was at this time that the organized study and collecting of shells emerged into a new science, conchology. However, collecting at this time continued to be focused on simply collecting and admiring these treasures.

Documenting the collected shells apparently began in the 17th century, when the field naturalist and Emperor Georg Eberhard Rumphius wrote a masterwork of natural history based on his observations. Rumphius conducted his studies at a trading post on the island of Ambon in the East Indies. A half century after his work, other scholars adopted some of the names he used to identify various mollusks.

During the 17th and 18th centuries, it was fashion-able for refined, educated Europeans to house and display their shell collections in entire rooms. Today, many outstanding collections are housed in national museums.

Scientific collecting became an earnest activity in the nineteenth century. Scientists actively studied mollusks and published books illustrating them. This newer malacology is the study of mollusks' biological functions, including how they make their shells.

Sharing Your Shells With Others

Friends and family will enjoy the interesting shelling discoveries you make and the beautiful souvenirs you bring home. Everyone seems to enjoy the wonders of nature, especially seashells of varying sizes, shapes, and colors. Simply give individual shells to others as souvenirs and gifts. We often give the organizations inviting us to speak a large whelk shell or sand dollar as a "thank you."

When organizing your shells, note the location you found the shells, along with the scientific and common name of the shell. This information is important when displaying your collection as an educational resource.

A cabinet with small drawers, each with dividers, makes an ideal sorting and storage case. Lay shells out in each drawer according to species and label each shell. If you number each shell, you can make a reference list containing additional information, including the location and conditions they were found in. A simpler method of storage is to put shells from the same location in one box. Label the box indicating where the shells were found and the date they were found. Use recycled plastic food containers for smaller species.

The easiest way to share your shells with others is to display them around your home, setting them out on a coffee table, end table, or fireplace mantle. You can border your garden with larger whelk shells or place them individually throughout the flowerbeds. Another effective display method is to put shells in clear glass containers. They are impressive looking when strategically displayed in unique containers such as old apothecary jars, large brandy snifters, mason jars, or in clear glass base table lamps. When filling the containers, place the best shells against the glass and fill the middle with cracked or broken shells, where they cannot be seen. By placing the shells carefully, you will not hide the good shells. Shadow boxes and recessed glass top tables also make interesting display cases.

Displaying your shell collection in public libraries, schools, or civic centers will provide you with a sense of pride and accomplishment. Larger collections of good quality shells make excellent educational exhibits. Shells and other beach collectibles displayed in a glass case should be labeled with their name and the location each item was found. Exhibiting your collection in an organized way enhances its beauty, and the viewing public will be in awe over the variety and uniqueness of your collection.

Another way to share your shells is to make interesting crafts with them. There are many books available providing directions and pictures of craft ideas. Some examples of shell crafts include shell refrigerator magnets, mirrors with shells glued on the frame, shell night lights, and grapevine wreaths decorated with shells. Homemade jewelry is also a popular way to display smaller shells. Earrings and pins can be made with shells using a little hot glue and recycling old inexpensive jewelry. Other shells are easily strung onto gold chains or ribbons to make necklaces.

Afterword

We hope you have enjoyed *The Art of Shelling*. Our purpose in writing this book was to share with others the joy we experience when shelling and observing nature. We wanted you to feel like you were really on the beach–smelling the fresh salt air, listening to the gulls, while searching for another treasure. Let us know how we did.

Happy Shelling!

Authors

Chuck and Debbie Robinson have been interested in seashells and the seashore since childhood. They both grew up on the New Jersey shore and together they have been combing beaches since 1984. The Robinsons have searched for seashells on United States East Coast beaches from Florida to Maine. They have also been shelling in Canada, the Bahamas, Bermuda, St. Martin, Hawaii, and in the United States Virgin Islands at St. Thomas and St. John.

The Robinsons began their writing careers with the first edition of *The Art of Shelling: A complete guide to finding shells and other beach collectibles at shelling locations from Florida to Maine* published in 1995. Their children's book *Treasure For Our Sand Castle* was published in 1997. Chuck and Debbie have both of their titles in slide format. They lecture extensively, presenting to schools, libraries, reading conferences, community organizations, and nature groups.

Chuck is a free lance newspaper photographer. He is also producing and marketing his seashore photography.

Debbie has a Bachelor of Arts Degree in Psychology and a Master of Science Degree in Education. She is the Director of Business Education and Training at Ocean County College, Toms River, New Jersey.

The Robinsons have a special interest in nature and are active with many nature groups to include the Ocean Nature and Conservation Society and the American Littoral Society. The Robinsons are members of The Bailey-Matthews Shell Museum, Sanibel Island, Florida and the Cape Cod Writers' Center.

Illustrator

April Wengren graduated Magna cum laude from Kutztown University, Kutztown Pennsylvania, with a Bachelor of Fine Arts degree in Painting. She also studied weaving and fiber design. This was the art form she focused on early in her career. After being honored with numerous awards for her weaving, April felt "the pull" to return to painting and two-dimensional design. She started illustrating in pen and ink and is known for her accurate, detailed drawings. April was the illustrator for the first edition of *The Art of Shelling* and the Robinsons' children's book, *Treasure For Our Sand Castle*. She continues working in pen and ink. April is also fascinated with color, which she explores through painting and mixed media.

Text Consultant

Dr. Judith Icklan made her debut in non-academic free lance editing with the first edition of *The Art of Shelling*. She holds Masters Degrees in English and in Reading Specialization and a Ph.D. in Rhetoric and Linguistics. The opportunity to work with the Robinsons' children's book *Treasure For Our Sand Castle* satisfied her particular interest in readability.

Dr. Icklan is the Associate Vice-President of Academic and Student Affairs at Ocean County College in Toms River, New Jersey.

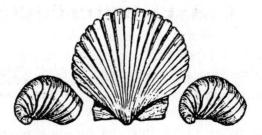

Travel References

FLORIDA

Bahia Honda State Park
36850 Overseas Hwy
Big Pine Key. FL 33043
305-872-2353

Bailey-Matthews Shell Museum
3075 Sanibel-Captiva Road
PO Box 1580
Sanibel. FL 33957
941-395-2233

Canaveral National Seashore
Park Headquarters
308 Julia Street
Titusville. FL 32796
407-267-1110
www.nps.gov/cana

Dania Beach Chamber
of Commerce. Greater
PO Box 1017
Dania. FL 33004
954-926-2323
email: greaterdania@
greaterdania.org
www.greaterdania.org

Dunedin Chamber of Commerce
301 Main Street
Dunedin. FL 34698
727-733-3198
email: chamber@dunedin-
fl.com
www.dunedin-fl.com

Florida Keys and Key West
Development Council
3406 North Roosevelt Blvd..
Suite 201
PO Box 866
Key West. FL 33041
800-FLA-Keys
305-296-1552

Florida State Parks
www.dep.state.fl.us/parks

Honeymoon Island
State Recreation Area
c/o Gulf Islands Goepark
#1 Causeway Blvd.
Dunedin. FL 34698
727-469-5942

J. N. "Ding" Darling National
Wildlife Refuge
1 Wildlife Drive
Sanibel. FL 33957-3032
941-472-1100
email: louishinds@fws.gov

John U. Lloyd Beach State
Recreation Area
6503 North Ocean Drive
Dania. FL 33004
954-923-2833

John Pennekamp Coral Reef
State Park
P.O. Box 487
Key Largo. FL 33037
305-451-1202

Lake Wales Area
  Chamber of Commerce
  340 West Central Ave.
  P.O. Box 191
  Lake Wales. FL 33859-0191
  863-676-3445
  email: lwacc@worldnet.
                    att.net
  www.lakewaleschamber.com

Long Key State Park
  P.O. Box 776
  Long Key. FL 33001
  305-664-4815

Lower Keys and Big Pine
  Chamber of Commerce
  P.O. Drawer 430511
  Big Pine. FL 33043-0511
  800-872-3722

Marathon Chamber of
  Commerce
  3330 Overseas Highway
  Marathon. FL 33050
  800-262-7284

Merritt Island
  National Wildlife Refuge
  P.O. Box 6504
  Titusville. FL 32782
  407-861-0667
  email: r4rw_fl.mrt@fws.gov
  http:\\merrittisland.fws.gov

Monroe County
  Tourist Development Council
  3406 N. Roosevelt Blvd.
  Key West. FL 33040
  305-296-1552
  800-352-5397
  www.fla-keys.com

Sanibel-Captiva Islands
  Chamber of Commerce
  1159 Causeway Road
  Sanibal. FL 33957
  941-472-1080

email: island@sanibel-
                    captiva.org
www.sanibel-captiva.org

Venice Area
  Chamber of Commerce
  257 Tamiami Trail North
  Venice. FL 34285
  941-488-2236
  207-255-4649
  email: vchamber@
                    venicechamber. com
  www.venicechamber.com

MAINE

Acadia National Park
  P.O. Box 177
  Bar Harbor. ME 04609
  207-288-3338
  www.nps.gov/acad

Bar Harbor
  Chamber of Commerce
  93 Cottage Street
  Bar Harbor. ME 04609
  207-288-5103
  email: bhcc@acadia.net
  www.barharborinfo.com

Downeast Coastal
  Chamber of Commerce
  PO Box 331
  Harrington. ME 04643
  207-483-4075
  email: downeast@
                    xoommail.com

Eastport Area
  Chamber of Commerce
  P.O. Box 254
  78 Water Street
  Eastport. ME 04631
  207-853-4644

Ellsworth Area
  Chamber of Commerce
  163 High Street

PO Box 267
Ellsworth. ME 04605
207-667-5584
email: eacc@downeast.net
http://w2.downeast.net/eacc

Machias Bay Area
Chamber of Commerce
P.O. Box 606
Machias. ME 04654
207-255-4402
www.nemaine.com/mbacc

Maine Tourism Association
325B Water Street
P.O. Box 2300
Hallowell. ME 04347
207-623-0363
www.mainetourism.com

Petit Manan
National Wildlife Refuge
P.O. Box 279
Milbridge. ME 04258-0279
Office: Water Street
207-546-2124
email: r5rw pmnwr@fws.gov
www.fws.gov/r5fws/me/
                    pmn.htm

Schoodic Peninsula
Chamber of Commerce
PO Box 381
Winter Harbor. ME 04693
800-231-3008
207-963-7658
email: info@acadia-
            schoodic.org
www.acadia.schoodic.org

MASSACHUSETTS

Cape Cod
Chamber of Commerce
P.O. Box 790
Hyannis. MA 02601
508-862-0700
888-332-2732

Office: 307 Main St.. Suite 2
Visitor Center: Junction US
Route 6 & Route 132

Cape Cod National Seashore
South Wellfleet. MA 02663
508-349-3785

Chatham Chamber of Commerce
P.O. Box 793
Chatham. MA 02633
508-945-5199
800-715-5567
email: chamber@
            chathamcapecod.org

Chatham Information Booth
533 Main Street
Chatham. MA 02633
508-945-5199
email: vacationinfo@
            state.ma.us

Eastham Chamber of Commerce
P.O. Box 1329
Eastham. MA 02642
508-240-7211

Massachusetts Office of
Travel & Tourism
State Transportation Bldg.
10 Park Place. Suite 4510
Boston. MA 02116
617-973-8500
800-227-MASS
www.mass-vacation.com/
                    index.shtml

Provencetown
Chamber of Commerce
P.O. Box 1017
307 Commercial Street
Provincetown. MA 02657-1017
508-487-3424
email: info@
            ptownchamber.com

NEW JERSEY

Barnegat Light. Borough of
   Municipal Building
   10 West 10th Street
   Barnegat Light. NJ 08006
   609-494-9196
   email: borohall@barnlight.com
   www.barnlight.com

Barnegat Lighthouse State Park
   PO Box 167
   Barnegat Light. NJ 08006
   609-494-2016
   www.state.nj.us/dep/forestry/
            parks/barnlig.htm

Belmar Chamber of Commerce
   1005½ Mainstreet
   Belmar. NJ 07719
   732-681-2900

Cape May Chamber of
   Commerce. Greater
   P.O. Box 556
   Cape May. NJ 08204
   609-884-5508
   email: ccgcm@
            algorithms.com
   www.capemaychambar.com

Cape May County
   Chamber of Commerce
   P.O. Box 74
   Cape May Court House.
   NJ 08210
   609-465-7181
   email: inquiry@cmccofc.com
   www.cmccofc.com

Cape May County
   Department of Tourism
   P.O. Box 365
   Cape May Court House.
   NJ 08210
   Office: #4 More Road
   Crest Haven Complex
   800-227-2297
   609-463-6415

Cape May-Lewes Ferry
   Sandman Blvd. & Lincoln Dr.
   North Cape May. NJ 08204
   302-644-6030 DE
   609-889-7200 NJ
   800-64 FERRY
   www.capemay-lewesferry.com

Division of Travel and Tourism
   New Jersey Travel Guide
   CN 826. 20 W. State Street
   Trenton. NJ 08625-0826
   800-JERSEY7

Gateway National
   Recreational Area
   Public Affairs Office
   Floyd Bennett Field. Bldg. 69
   Brooklyn. NY 11234
   732-872-5970 (Sandy Hook)
   www.nps.gov/gate

Manasquan
   Chamber of Commerce
   107 Main Street
   Manasquan. NJ 08736
   732-223-8303

New Jersey Coastal
   Heritage Trail
   National Park Service
   PO Box 568
   Newport. NJ 08345

OUTER BANKS, NORTH CAROLINA

National Park Service
   Cape Hatteras National
      Seashore
   Route 1. Box 675
   Manteo. NC 27954
   252-473-2111
   www.nps.gov/caha/
            capehatteras.html

Outer Banks
  Chamber of Commerce
  P.O. Box 1757
  101 Town Hall Drive
  Kill Devil Hills. NC 27948
  252-441-8144
  email: chamber@outer-
              banks.com
  www.outerbankschamber.com

VIRGINIA

Assateague Island
  National Seashore
  7206 National Seashore Lane
  Berlin. MD 21811-9742
  410-641-1441
  410-641-3030

Chesapeake Bay Bridge-Tunnel
  P.O. Box 111
  Cape Charles. VA 23310-0111
  757-331-2960
  www.cbbt.com

Chincoteague
  Chamber of Commerce
  P.O. Box 258
  Chincoteague. VA 23336
  757-336-6161
  email: pony@
              shore.intercom.net

Chincoteague
  National Wildlife Refuge
  US Fish and Wildlife Service
  PO Box 62
  8231 Beach Road
  Chincoteague. VA 23336-0062
  757-336-6122
  email: rsrw chnwr@fws.gov
  http://chinco.fws.gov

Bibliography

Abbott, R. Tucker. *Kingdom of the Seashell*. New York: Crown Publishers, Inc., 1998.

Abbott, R. Tucker and Robert E. Lipe. *Living Shells of the Caribbean and Florida Keys*. Melbourne, Florida: American Malacologists, Inc., 1991.

Abbott, R. Tucker. *Seashells of the World*. New York: Western Publishing Company, Inc, 1985.

Alexander, John and James Lazell. *RIBBON OF SAND: The Amazing Convergence of the Ocean and the Outer Banks*. Chapel Hill, North Carolina: Algonquin Books of Chapel Hill, 1992.

Ballance, Alton. *Ocracokers*. Chapel Hill: The University of North Carolina Press, 1989.

Bergeron, Eugene. *How to Clean Seashells*. St. Petersburg, Florida: Great Outdoors Publishing Co., 1971.

Bragg, Cecil. *OCRACOKE ISLAND: PEARL OF THE OUTER BANKS*. Manteo, N.C.: Times Printing Co., Inc., 1973.

Chesterman, Charles W. *The Audubon Society Field Guide to North American Rocks and Minerals.* New York: Alfred A. Knopf, Inc., 1978.

D'Amato, Albert C. and Miriam F. d'Amato. *Maine Itineraries: Discovering the Down East Region, Scenic, Historical, and Cultural Sites Along Route 1 from Ellsworth to Calais.* Winthrop, MA: Professional Editorial Service, Inc., 1987.

Eastern National Park & Monument Association. *Acadia National Park Motorists' Guide.* Bar Harbor, ME: Acadia Publishing Company, 1989.

Florida Department of Natural Resources, Division of Recreation and Parks. *Florida State Parks...the Real Florida.*

Florida Department of Natural Resources, Division of Recreation and Parks. *Honeymoon Island State Recreation Area...More of the Real Florida.*

Fodor's Travel Publications, Inc. *Fodor's 93 Florida.* New York: Fodor's Travel Publications, Inc., 1992.

Kane, Joseph Nathan, Steven Anzovin and Janet Podell. *Facts About the States.* New York: The H.W. Wilson Company, 1989.

Kendel, David L. *Glaciers & Granite: A Guide to Maine's Landscape & Geology.* Camden, Maine: Down East Books, 1987.

Manley, Robert and Seon Manley. *beaches: their lives, legends, and lore.* Philadelphia: Chilton Book Company, 1968.

Meinkoth, Norman A. *The Audubon Society Field Guide to North American Seashore Creatures*. New York: Alfred A, Knopf, Inc., 1981.

National Geographic Society. *National Geographic Traveler. Vol. IX, Number 3*. Washington, DC: National Geographic Society, 1992.

National Geographic Society. *National Geographic Traveler. Vol. IX, Number 6*. Washington, DC: National Geographic Society, 1992.

National Geographic Society. *National Geographic Traveler. Vol. XI, Number 2*. Washington, DC: National Geographic Society, 1994.

National Geographic Society. *National Geographic's Guide to the National Parks of the United States*. Washington D.C.: National Geographic Society, 1989.

National Park Service. *Assateague Island*. Washington D.C.: U.S. Department of the Interior, 1985.

Nordstrom, Karl F., Paul A. Gares, Norbert P. Psuty, Orrin H. Pilkey, Jr., William J. Neal and Orrin H. Pilkey, Sr. *Living with the New Jersey Shore*. Durham, N.C.: Duke University Press, 1986.

Readers Digest Association, Inc. *North American Wildlife*. New York: Readers Digest Association, Inc. 1983.

Readers Digest Association, Inc. *Off The Beaten Path*. United States of America: Readers Digest Association, Inc., 1987.

Rehder, Harald. *The Audubon Society Field Guide To North American Seashells*. New York: Alfred A. Knopf, 1981.

Richardson, Frederick C. *Seashells of Cape Cod National Seashore*. Eastham, MA: Eastern National Park and Monument Association, 1987.

Shears, David. *Ocracoke: Its History and People*. Washington, D.C.: Starfish Press, 1992.

Smithsonian Books. *The Native Americans*. Atlanta, GA: Turner Publishing, Inc., 1993.

Sowerby, Jr., G.B. *Sowerby's Book of Shells*. NY: Crescent Books, 1990.

Spitsbergen, Judith. *SEACOAST LIFE: An Ecological Guide to Natural Seashore Communities in North Carolina*. Chapel Hill: The University of North Carolina Press, 1980.

Stahly, Greg, and Shelley Stahly. *The Sand Dollar*. Marco Island, Florida: The Artisian, 1981.

Stix, Hugh, Marguerite Stix and R. Tucker Abbott. *THE SHELL: Five Hundred Million Years of Inspired Design*. NY: Harry N. Abrams, Inc. Publishers, 1988.

Walker, Cyril, and David Ward. *Fossils*. New York, NY: Dorling Kindersley, Inc., 1992.

Williams, Carol. *Beach Bountiful: Southeast*. Jacksonville Beach, Florida: Pegasus Medallion Press, 1993.

Williams, Winston. *Florida's Fabulous Seashells and Seashore Life*. Tampa, Florida: World Publications, 1998.

Zinn, Donald. *THE HANDBOOK FOR BEACH STROLLERS: from Maine to Cape Hatteras, 2nd ed.* Chester, Connecticut: The Globe Pequot Press, 1985.

Index

NOTES

NOTES

NOTES

NOTES